Pietas

Pietas

An Introduction to Roman Traditionalism
Second Edition

Giuseppe Barbera

Translated by Ilenia Contessa

Mythology Corner : Wilmington

Published in 2021 by Mythology Corner, Wilmington 19807

© 2021 by Mythology Corner (Second Edition, English)

All rights reserved. Except as permitted under the United States Copyright Act of 1976, no part of this publication may be reproduced, stored in a retrieval system, or transmitted in any form or by any means, electronic, mechanical, photocopying, recording, or otherwise without the prior written permission of Mythology Corner.

ISBN 978-0-9817596-1-6 (Paperback)

ISBN 978-0-9817596-3-0 (ePub)

First Edition Published in 2014 by Giuseppe Barbera

© 2014 by Giuseppe Barbera (First Edition, Italian)

First Edition Title - Aspetti Esoterici nella Tradizione Romana Gentile

First Edition ISBN 978-8-8264254-3-6 (Paperback)

First Edition ISBN 978-6-0503406-4-8 (ePub, Kindle)

Mythology Corner acknowledges Mr. Stefano Sogari for introducing the author to them and acknowledges Mr. Catanzaro and the author for the Latin translation of the publisher's note. The author acknowledges the entire Pietas community for their valuable support and help in publishing this book.

Images on pages 2, 8, 18, 30, 34, 41, 48, 51, 63, 75, 79, 86, 88, 94, 96, 102, 106, 111, 113, 118, and 128 and the Appendix 4 are not copyrighted by Mythology Corner. They are reproduced in this book under either the public domain or various types of Creative Commons licenses as noted in the caption below the images or text on these pages, respectively.

Publisher's Cataloging-In-Publication Data

(Prepared by The Donohue Group, Inc.)

Names: Barbera, Giuseppe, 1981- author. | Contessa, Ilenia, translator.
Title: Pietas : an introduction to Roman Traditionalism / Giuseppe Barbera ; translated by Ilenia Contessa.
Other Titles: Aspetti esoterici nella Tradizione Romana Gentile. English
Description: Second edition. | Wilmington [Delaware] : Mythology Corner, 2021. | Translation of: Aspetti esoterici nella Tradizione Romana Gentile. | Includes bibliographical references and index.
Identifiers: ISBN 9780981759616 (paperback) | ISBN 9780981759630 (ePub)
Subjects: LCSH: Italy--Religion. | Italians--Religious life. | Paganism--Italy. | Romans--Italy--Religion.
Classification: LCC BL980.I8 B3713 2021 (print) | LCC BL980.I8 (ebook) | DDC 200.945--dc23

www.mythologycorner.com

To our spiritual guide, my teacher and my father, Gianfranco Barbera

Except for the Publisher's Note, all information, including facts, analyses, and opinions presented in this book, are of the author, Mr. Giuseppe Barbera's only and not of Mythology Corner or Rays LLC or anyone else.

Indigenous peoples have the right to manifest, practice, develop and teach their spiritual and religious traditions, customs and ceremonies; the right to maintain, protect, and have access in privacy to their religious and cultural sites; the right to the use and control of their ceremonial objects; and the right to the repatriation of their human remains.

United Nations Declaration on the Rights of Indigenous Peoples - Article 12.1

Everyone has the right to freedom of thought, conscience and religion. This right includes freedom to change religion or belief and freedom, either alone or in community with others and in public or in private, to manifest religion or belief, in worship, teaching, practice and observance.

EU Charter of Fundamental Rights - Article 10.1

All religious denominations shall be equally free before the law.

Constitution of the Italian Republic - Article 8.1

Contents

Abbreviations	xv
Nota Publisherae	xvii
De Introductione	**1**
Introduction	3
De Traditionis Romanae Origine	**7**
Romulus	9
The *Pomerium* and the Walls	17
The Square Rome	21
The Doors	25
The Palace	28
The Temple of Vesta	31
De Pietate et religione	**33**
Understanding *Pietas*	**35**
The Temple	39
Esoterism and Exoterism	44
The Art of Haruspex	47
Sacerdotal Colleges	50
Functions of the Pontifical College	53
Clavus Annalis	58
De Initiationis Mysteriisque	**61**
Introduction	62
Initiation	66
Practicing Roman Religion Today	72
The Mysteries	82

The First Mystery	83
The Mysteries of Hercules	85
The Mysteries of Saturn	89

De Mytho — 93

Sacred Literature	95
Perseus	98
Problems in Myth Interpretation	100
Jason and the Golden Fleece	107
Aeneid, Eclogues and Georgics	109
Iliad and Odyssey	112

De Magia — 117

Magic	119

De Pietate Fama Societate — 123

Pietas, from Antiquity to Today	125
Pietas Organization	134

Appendices — 151

Appendix 1: Roman Chronology	152
Appendix 2: *Pietas* Calendar	166
Appendix 3: Selected Roman Deities	183
Appendix 4: Of the Wonderful Natures of Fire and Earth	192

Glossary — 194

Bibliography — 200

Notes — 201

Index — 205

About Author — 221

Illustrations

Emperor Marcus Aurelius (161-180 AD) and members of the Imperial family offer sacrifice in gratitude for success against Germanic tribes. Bas-relief from the Arch of Marcus Aurelius, Rome, now in the Capitoline Museum in Rome.   2

Ceremony at the Jupiter temple of the Pietas Gentile Community in Rome, Italy.   4

Schematic map of Rome showing the seven hills.   8

Bartolomeo Pinelli, Romulus traces the borders of Rome with the plow, 1835.   18

Temples along Via Sacra's sinuous route from Capitoline Hill to Coliseum are understood as microcosmic projections of the seven major celestial planets.   22

Temple of the Divo Romulo, Rome.   26

Lasha Tskhondia, A derivative work of a 3D model - L.VII.C   30

Pietas is not religion but a sacred duty to the Gods, the ancestors, the country, family, and friends.   34

Guillaume Rouille, Numa Pompilus.   41

The temple's form is derived from the idea of reorganizing the four elements of nature. Each side of the temple indicates a distinct element of nature, and the space within it is permeated by the remaining fifth element, which is the essence that allows contact between the human and divine world. Likewise, the man is made up of the same four basic elements, earth is his body, air is his mind, water is his soul and fire is his spirit.   45

Wilhelm Deecke, Diagram of the bronze liver of Piacenza.   48

Flamines, distinguished by their pointed apices, as part of a procession on the Augustan Altar of Peace   51

Shakko, Relief found in Neumagen near Trier, a teacher with three discipuli. Around 180–185 CE. Photo of casting in Pushkin museum, Moscow.   63

An initiate under the guidance of a teacher goes through the lunar and solar phases of education.   68

Claus Ableiter, Lararium (Sacrificial altar and niche for figurines of Gods), found in Pompeii, 79 AD.   75

Lararium of a Modern-Day Pietas Adherent   77

Unknown, Photograph of a first-century Roman Lararium from the House of the Vettii in Pompeii. The astral serpent at the bottom represents Genius Loci.   79

Marie-Lan Nguyen, Front panel from a sarcophagus with the Labours of Heracles: from left to right, the Nemean Lion, the Lernaean Hydra, the Erymanthian Boar, the Ceryneian

Hind, the Stymphalian birds, the Girdle of Hippolyta, the Augean stables, the Cretan Bull and the Mares of Diomedes. Luni marble, Roman artwork from the middle 3rd century CE. 86

Carole Raddato, Saturn with head protected by winter cloak, holding a scythe in his right hand, fresco from the House of the Dioscuri at Pompeii, Naples Archaeological Museum. 88

The doctor Japyx heals Aeneas (sided by his mother, Goddess Venus, and by his own son Ascanius, who is weeping), wounded on one leg. Ancient Roman fresco from the "House of Sirico" in Pompeii, Italy); mid 1st century. On display at the Museo Archeologico Nazionale (Naples). 94

Julius Troschel, Perseus and Andromeda, Neue Pinakothek in Munich, around 1840/50. 96

Benvenuto Cellini, Perseus, Loggia dei Lanzi, Florence, Italy. 102

Marie-Lan Nguyen, Pelias, king of Iolcos, stops on the steps of a temple as he recognises young Jason by his missing sandal. 106

Jean-Baptiste Wicar, Virgil reading the Aeneid to Augustus, Octavia, and Livia. 111

Johann Heinrich Wilhelm Tischbein, Odysseus and Penelope. 113

Marie-Lan Nguyen, Magical book formed of seven pages enclosed by a cover with a veiled woman's head and a bearded man. 118

Ignota, Giuliano Kremmerz, 1890. 128

Gianfranco Barbera, the spiritual guide of the founders of the Pietas organization. 135

Gianfranco's artwork in Crotone's provincial building depicting foundation of ancient Kroton. 137

Gianfranco's artwork in Crotone's provincial building depicting Pythogarean school in ancient Kroton. 138

Pietas Temple of Goddess Minerva in Pordenone, Italy 143

Pietas Temple of God Apollo in Palermo, Italy 144

Pietas Temple of God Apollo in Ardea, Italy 145

Pietas Temple of God Jupiter in Rome, Italy 146

Abbreviations

B.C.E - Before Common Era

C.E. - Common Era

ab U.c. - Anno urbis conditae

Nota Publisherae

Praeteritae quattuor decade ortum et celere de ethnicis religionibus studiorum in academiis incrementum viderunt. Omnia propria quae de religionibus studiorum argumentum definiunt, insuper collectaneis a paribus inspectis ephemeridibus, annuis consiliis, propriam parte in Civitatum Foederatarum Religionum Academia et eminentibus in Universali Relgionum Senatu legatis habet. Discriminans arte factum in humanarum litterarum studiis impedimentum, quod vera pervestigatio sola de aequa *vis*ione ex longinquo gignatur, omnino deletum est et scientia per multa saecula celata ex imis totius orbi consuetudinibus erupit. Hic thesaurus non solum de religionibus studia, sed etiam omnem litterarum humanarum academicum locum auxit. In Europa hic progressus praecipue familiariter homines inter omnes ethnicas continentis religiones, a slavicis Russicis consuetudinibus ad Celticum morem Druidarum in Hibernia, ab Asatru in Suecia ad Hellenismum in Graecia, utendi incremento ductus est. Fere quinquaginta praeteritis annis hae gentes ex occultis conventionibus orate sunt ad templa aedificanda, ut multos homines in publicis locis congregarent. Localia, provincialia et patria per Europam imperia et internationals societates, insuper Europaea Unioni et Foederatis Nationibus, iam rationes habent ad necessariam praecipuis religiosis iuribus tutelam servandam vel operam cum his consuetudinibus sociant, qui praesentes defectus corrigent. Media, ipsa societas et etiam scientifica consortio ea in hodierni mundi pluribus cultibus compositi partibus admiserunt. Hic liber rationalis consequentia est huius motus et adherentibus Romanae Usitatae Religioni in Italia vox est. Auctor facta et explicationes cum quadam audacia et narratione adiungit, ut breviter vastam rem in hoc proemii opere ostendat. Unicum modum in hoc genere praebet, rem tali modo explicans ut opus simul academicis, laicis lectoribus et huic fidei adhaerentibus scilicet utile sit. Hic liber commoda ratio omnium humanarum litterarum studiosorum est, insuper illis in sedibus de antiquis litteris, qui nova petunt, magistris studiorum cursus munera administrantibus ad semper fecundas huic rei e discipulorum societatibus flagitationes satisfaciendas, et scholiis, ipsis discipulis, Romanae Usitatae fidei adhaerentibus, qui simplicem ducem poscunt, et aliis gentium totum per mundum religionibus, quae experientiis sociarum in Italia frui volunt. Mythology Corner hoc opus ad forum volup edit et sperat fore ut coniuncte operam cum sortes habentibus societ ad perpetuum utrique salubre auxilium. Speramus vos hoc libro legendo gavisuros et utilem ad artem et ad vitam privatam exsistimaturos esse.

Publisher's Note

The last four decades have seen the emergence and steady growth of ethnic religious studies in academia. It has all the major characteristics that define a religious studies subject, including peer-reviewed journals, annual conferences, a dedicated unit in the American Academy of Religions, and a visible contingent at the World Parliament of Religions. The discriminatorily selective artificial constraint in humanities that genuine research stems only from an objective non-adherent point of view has finally been consigned to the dustbin, and centuries of hidden knowledge has gushed out from the insiders of all traditions around the world. This treasure has significantly enriched not just religious studies but the entire humanities academic space. In Europe, this trend was driven primarily by the phenomenal growth in practicing membership within every ethnic faith of the continent, from Slavic traditions in Russia to Celtic Druidism in Ireland and from Asatru in Sweden to Hellenism in Greece. In the last twenty or so years, these groups have come out from practicing in secrecy to building temples and holding large gatherings in public spaces. Local, provincial, and national governments across Europe and the international organizations, including the European Union and the United Nations, either already have the framework to provide the necessary protection of their fundamental religious rights or are working with these traditions to remedy any gaps therein. The media, society in general, and even the scientific community have come to accept them as part and parcel of our multicultural world today. This book is a natural consequence of this great movement and is the voice of the adherents of the Roman Traditional Religion in Italy. The author combines facts and analyses with a dash of passion and storytelling to succinctly present a vast subject matter in this short introductory work. He demonstrates a unique style in this genre by presenting the content in a manner such that the work is at once useful for academics, lay readers, and of course, the adherents of his faith. This book is an excellent resource for researchers across humanities, including those in the classics department who are looking for fresh ideas, educators designing course work for satisfying the ever-growing demand for this subject from their student communities at not only the universities but also schools, the students themselves, adherents of the Roman traditional faith seeking a basic guide and for other ethnic faiths around the world who want to benefit from the experiences of their counterparts in Italy. Mythology corner is delighted to bring this wonderful work to the market and looks forward to collaborating closely with all stakeholders in this space for a continued mutually beneficial engagement. We hope you will enjoy reading this book and find it useful both professionally and personally.

Capitulum I
De Introductione

Emperor Marcus Aurelius (161-180 AD) and members of the Imperial family offer sacrifice in gratitude for success against Germanic tribes. Bas-relief from the Arch of Marcus Aurelius, Rome, now in the Capitoline Museum in Rome.

MatthiasKabel, CC BY-SA 3.0, <https://creativecommons.org/licenses/by-sa/3.0/deed.en>, via Wikipedia Commons.

Introduction

This book is about one of the fastest-growing religious communities, if not the fastest, in Italy today, namely the ancient Roman tradition. A shared tradition of those simple shepherds, who established the first square city among the famous seven hills of present-day Rome. The same tradition that centuries later gave birth to Rome, the center of the great Roman civilization of which so much is spoken of and imagined even today. Even after its demise, this civilization continues to live within the hearts and minds of all Europeans wherever they may be. It reincarnated itself again and again, in the ambitions of conquerors who attempted to recreate the Roman Empire and in the ideas of ordinary citizens who imagined themselves in the image of ***Cives Romanus***[1] through their arts, architecture, philosophy, and overall way of life. Who can deny Charlemagne's explicit recall to ancient Rome on the eve of his coronation as Emperor of Rome, or the Germanic dynasties of the Holy Roman Empire, or the last masterpiece that the Enlightenment gave birth in France, which started as a republic and then, like Rome itself, became imperial? Who would not agree in calling Napoleon the last Roman emperor, the last one who tried to form a Roman Empire of Europe and Africa, who had the audacity to have a sculpture of his made depicting himself as the Roman God Mars and who called, in his vainglorious hopes, the tenderest fruits of his love, King of Rome! Nor should we forget the last ephemeral adventure carried on by Fascist Italy, which, with the conquest of Ethiopia, attempted to form an empire in the image of Rome's dream. Isn't it true that our lands are impregnated with the blood of all those young soldiers who dreamed about the greatness of Rome while they carried imperial eagles in their battles?

The idea behind this book has no such grandiose aspirations but only a simple desire of being an ideal framework for all who seek to follow that ancient Roman tradition. Firstly, the book sheds light on the tradition itself from the perspective of the insider living the tradition today. Secondly, it explores the mindset and perception of the ancient Romans, especially that of the Roman patricians, who were the keepers of this tradition's

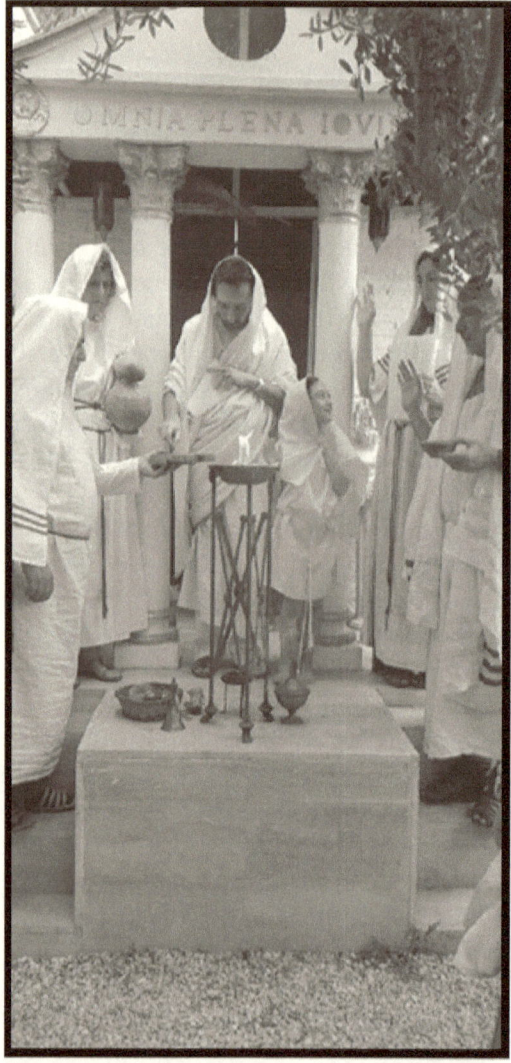

Ceremony at the Jupiter temple of the Pietas Gentile Community in Rome, Italy.

knowledge. Lastly, the book presents case studies to illustrate the tradition's interpretation of Roman mythology, which started from its own original culture and, along the way, absorbed and incorporated other mythologies that it encountered. This cumulation of traditions was natural given that the ancient **Urbe**[2] was one of the first real cosmopolitan cities of the world, open to other traditions, except those that were perceived as immoral. For example, the Bacchanalia were forbidden[3]. Thus, it equips today's seeker of this ancient tradition with a foundation to correctly understand its cultural, social, political, and religious characteristics. Such a perspective is essential given that today's paradigms are not suitable for understanding this tradition correctly. Many historians have mocked our ancestors by saying that our ancestors made fundamental decisions for the state by interpreting the flights of birds or the pecking of sacred chickens on the **Collis Capitolinus**. Yet as long as the rules of **Pietas**[4] were respected, the Roman Empire met the two spouses **Gloria** and **Honor**[5], and only after the reprehensible abandonment of its tradition in the public state worship, the conjunction of decadence and dishonor made their appearance. And let us not even mention how fear was used to keep our people ignorant about their ancient traditions because that fear-based miseducation is still continuing.

Right after this introductory chapter, we dive into this path's mythological history in chapter 2, **De Traditionis Romanae Origine**. Here we will get to know King Romulus, learn about Rome's sacred beginnings, touch upon its esoteric architecture and understand the importance of the holy fire and the Temple of Vesta. The next chapter discusses the crucial distinction between **Pietas** and religion. In this chapter, which is aptly titled **De Pietate et Religione**, we will talk about the temples and study the organizational structure of the pontifical offices, along with few other related topics. Then we will enter the heart of the tradition's practices, namely initiations and mysteries, in chapter 4, **De Initiationis Mysteriisque**. In the following chapter, **De Mytho**, we will understand the correct interpretation of Roman mythology. We then get a brief glimpse into the tradition's magical practices in chapter 6, **De Magia**. Finally, we will end our journey with some closing words learning about our organization, *Associazione Tradizionale* **Pietas**, in the final chapter, **De Pietate Fama Societate**.

Whoever travels on the Roman Tradition's path of self-discovery, if her studies are sincere enough and her soul is uncorrupted, she will meet the Gods living inside her. At that juncture, questioning monotheism or polytheism will no longer be relevant, for she will understand that woman herself creates every deity, and when she has a clear vision of everything, she will admire the Roman Tradition for the wisdom that it has concealed in its mythology.

Capitulum II
De Traditionis Romanae Origine

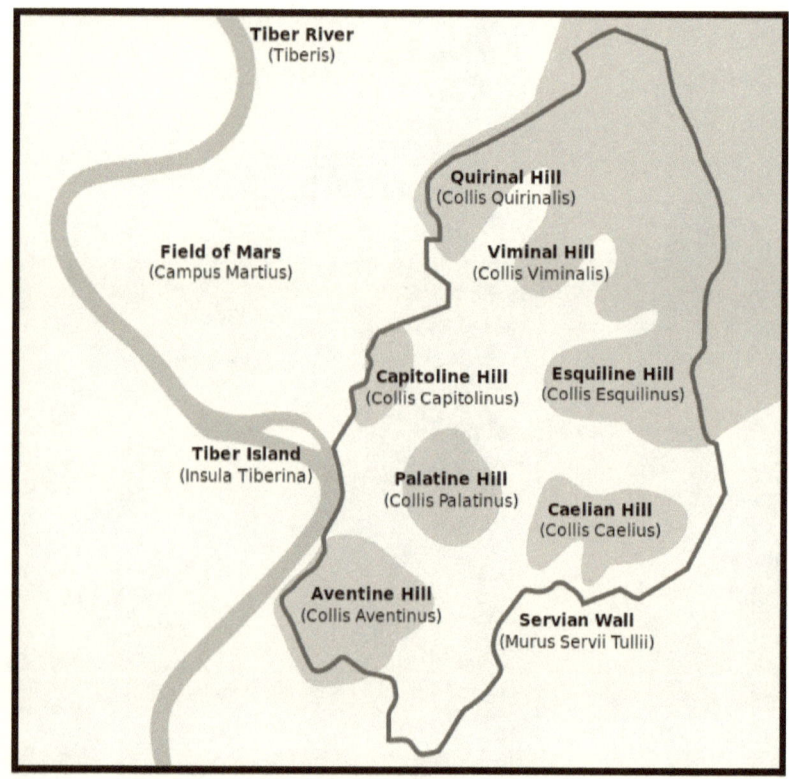

Schematic map of Rome showing the seven hills.

Renata3, CC BY-SA 4.0 <https://creativecommons.org/licenses/by-sa/4.0>, via Wikimedia Commons.

Romulus

It would seem logical to attribute to the birth of the city of Rome also that of its tradition, but the Roman tradition is older than the city of Rome. It evolved[6] as a syncretic product of various cultures over a long time, similar to the evolution of its closely related and contemporary Etruscan tradition[7]. To put a perspective on the historical time we are talking about, the first traces of settlements in the urban hills date back to approximately 18th century B.C.E., and the walls found on the Palatine hill are from 750 B.C.E. to 725 B.C.E[8]. The last excavations carried out on the Palatine slopes by the La Sapienza University of Rome show a succession of stratified activities, which provide evidence of this evolution and the mythological story[9] of this ancient city's birth. According to history, Rome emerged from the unification of preexisting proto-urban **Pagi**[10]. Since the Early Bronze Age, various **Pagi** existed on the seven hills, collectively known as the **Septimontium**. Over time one of them, namely the Palatine **Pagus**, dominated the others and became the nerve center of all the **Pagi** and eventually became Rome. From the excavations made in the area, Carandini authoritatively identified Rome's first palace. That there indeed was a first king of Rome is without a doubt true. Now, whether his name was Romulus and whether he had or not a twin brother is for archaeologists irrelevant because this subject falls in the field of mythology. A mythological model is associated with this unification based on Roman and Etruscan rituals related to the laying of foundations and inaugurations of new towns.[11] There are similar mythological models associated with other pre-Roman states that arose as conglomerations or, in any case, coeval to the first half of the 8th century B.C.E., from that of Alba to that of Ausculum.[12] The Roman mythology is a historical memory that has been enriched with symbols and is the source material for our theory of what we call myth-history for lack of a better word.

According to our tradition, Rome's founding fathers, the twins Romulus and Remus, were born in Alba Longa, one of the ancient cities near Rome's future site. Their mother, Rhea Silvia, was a Vestal Virgin. She was the daughter of the former king, Numitor. Amulius, brother of Numitor, had displaced Numitor and usurped his throne. Rhea Silvia conceives the twins when their father, the God Mars, visits her in a sacred grove dedicated to him. Seeing them as a possible threat to his rule, King Amulius orders the twins to be killed, and they are abandoned on the bank of the river Tiber to die. However, Tiberinus, the God of the Tiber river, finds them and gives them to the she-wolf Lupa, who had just lost her cubs to suckle. Eventually adopted by a shepherd, they grow up tending flocks, unaware of their true identities. When they are young adults, they become involved in a dispute between supporters of Numitor and Amulius. In the process, Remus is captured and brought to Alba Longa. Both their grandfather, Numitor, and king Amulius suspect his true identity. Romulus, meanwhile, organizes an effort to free his brother and sets out with help for Alba Longa. During this period, the twins learn of their past, join forces with their grandfather Numitor, and restore him to the throne after killing Amulius.

The twins then return and decide to build a city of their own but cannot agree on the location. Romulus prefers the Palatine Hill, above the Lupercal, but Remus wants to build on the Aventine Hill. To resolve the dispute, they agree to seek the Gods' approval through a contest of augury. Remus first sees six auspicious birds, but Romulus supersedes him when he sees twelve and claims divine approval for his plan. Romulus then inaugurates the construction of a walled city by ritually furrowing the ground and thereby drawing the perimeter close to which the city walls are to be built. This furrow had a magical value, and even if the wall had not yet been built, crossing it was a sacrilege. The penalty for this transgression was death. Remus, irritated by the divine favor towards Romulus, crosses the furrow to denigrate his brother's work, and despite the relationship of kinship between them, Remus paid with his own life. Romulus then establishes the city of Rome, its institutions, government, military, and religious traditions and reigns as its first king for many years.

So, what is Rome, and why does it charm us even today? It would have been an ambitious attempt to answer these questions here in this book but for our rigorous study and practice of the Roman Tradition for more than a generation now. To uncover its secrets, we must go deeper into the story of Romulus and do an esoteric analysis of Rome's origins only through which the Roman ideal materialized itself while enchanting millions of men in the process. First, we have to understand the divine sign that led to the city's foundation. The heavenly sign is the omen drawn by Romulus using augury, which resulted in his vision of the twelve vultures. Generally, the word vulture has a negative connotation because it is a bird that feeds on carcasses, but the word for vultures in the old world was ***Accipitridae***, which biologically includes hawks, goshawks, eagles, the common plains hawks, harriers, and kites. These birds are considered sacred. Goshawks are sacred to Mars, eagles to Jupiter, common plains hawks to Sun, harriers to Venus, and kites to Mercury. They fly high in the sky over long distances and are distinguishable by their common traits of having broad wings with rounded ends. The esoteric meaning behind this augury is that omens reflect the desire of the heavens. Rome was founded as per an Indo-European ritual, which was often the practice found in the ancient Iranian and Anatolian cities. At that time, the idea that the sky wants to project itself onto the earth was a well-established belief. It represents the inwardly reordering of men, that is, the "squaring of the circle." In fact, the ***Pomerium***, the city's sacred boundary, has a square shape, but the city walls are circular. The circle represents the human beings in their complexity, and the square the separation, distinction, and regularization of their four elements. This geometric principle applies not only to humans but also to all aspects of nature here on earth, and in fact, to the entire Cosmos. What specific bird had been sighted by Romulus is uncertain, for the literary sources give the simple definition of ***Accipitridae***. Maybe the whole class of these birds was eligible for the avian interpretation of good omens, which promised leadership and greatness.

While we cannot go into the details of avian augural interpretations for our discussion purposes, it would suffice to say that both Romulus and Remus received a solar sign. Remus saw six birds and Romulus twelve but Remus saw his omen before Romulus. The ancients interpreted this omen by concluding that if Remus ruled, he would obtain success for the city sooner, but the city would only be half as great as compared to its glory if Romulus ruled, even though for Romulus it would take more time to achieve that greater glory. When Romulus saw the twelve birds later, Remus was astonished, and he asked Romulus to point to the area where he saw the twelve birds. The future king pointed at a corner of the heavens where he had seen his omen, and all the birds he had seen reappeared there for all to see. Thus, the heavenly message was more favorable to Romulus. Plutarch confirms the divine origin of Romulus and the favor of the Gods for his work in his writings where he says, "Rome could not rise to such power if it had not, in some way, divine origin, such as to offer, in the eyes of men, something great and inexplicable."

Next, we delve into what Romulus did once he was chosen as the king to prepare the people of the area for this great work. Before we do that, we should understand the idea inherent in the word **Amor**, the flame that burned in the hearts of Rome's citizens. This divine and superior love is possible because of justice, which manifests through laws, and it is this that Rome shared with the world. Roman civilization aimed for true **Amor** among men by bringing justice amongst them because, more than anything else, what we desire from the depths of our souls is justice. It is not surprising why the righteous and pious men have always felt attracted by Rome. This divine love fueled by justice drew them to it, and it is the same that continues to charm us even today. To realize a large project, such as bringing justice among men, Romulus needed a group of spiritually evolved people. Normally that would require a long time to achieve, but Romulus, who had the divine favor of Jupiter, wanted to establish the city during this auspicious period, and therefore he initiated the citizens with a powerful and sacred fire ritual. This catharsis ritual of regeneration made it possible for the citizens to skip the lengthy period of initiation. Romulus knew that once the city was established, the initiation of their descendants would be more structured. Their fathers would train them in the path of the secrets of Rome, and after having reached the seventeenth year of age, they would ritually don the ***toga*** to embody the **Amor** of the Romans. So, their training would take place over time, but the seeds of the great city had to be sown right then. He had the confidence in the capabilities of his men, trust in the pact they had made with him, their deep faith in his divine vision of that great city Rome and in the sacred ritual he conducted for them. Together all this turned their spirits into a powerful igneous force ready to be connected to the sacred flame of **Amor**.

Civis Romanus sum implies being connected to the sacred fire of

Rome. The physical embodiment of this **Amor** was the fire temple in the center of the holy city and, to some extent, the fire the citizens maintained at their homes. Every year the fire was renewed with the new spring, led by the matrons of the house, and guarded there. In the Roman **Domus**, people warmed up with the sacred fire, they ate food cooked on it, they poured offers for the Gods into it, they loved each other in its presence. The life of the Roman man was deeply sacral in every gesture. The fire was one, and it was all the Gods at the same time. It allowed the Romans to relate to the Gods and live with them, tying every family to the same magical experience and divine ideal that connected them to the fire of the **Urbe**, guarded by pure virgins, for the idea to remain pure.

Reflecting this heavenly and divine love on earth was the task entrusted to the society founded by Romulus: Rome. This divine love was established through a fire ritual performed after the shepherds were initiated for this task. As for him, having placed himself at the head of the entire sacred function, he took a sacred trumpet - the Romans are used to calling it "lituus" from litè, "prayer" - he made it resound over the name of the city. The city had three names, an initiatory one, a sacred one, and a political one. Each of the three names has a specific purpose. The initiatory name is Amor, which means **eros**, and it was chosen so that everyone was pervaded by a divine love for the city, the reason for which the poet in the bucolic poems enigmatically calls it "Amaryllis." The sacred name is Flora, which means "flourishing," hence the festival of Floralia in her honor. Lastly, the political name is Roma. That single fire kept in the temple of Vesta and distributed to all families is, therefore, the unique God Amor that manifests itself in many forms. Romulus had founded the religion of true love. Aware of this, the greatest minds of antiquity hailed the miracles of love in many ways that ranged from ***nihil difficile amanti puto*** to the ***omnia vincit Amor et nos cedamus amori***.

In establishing this sacred city, Romulus studied the method of purification from guilt and founded the asylum: the mechanism of forgiveness of one's crimes in exchange for giving faith to Rome and committing oneself to the realization of the new society based on justice, and its occult and manifest fire. Romulus first realizes the ideal of forgiveness in exchange for a commitment to do what is right. He thus demonstrates that he has a profound knowledge of the divine laws and knows that a just and pious man can, with a simple healthy volitional commitment, redeem his errors before Jupiter, the God of Law. Romulus established that sacrifice burns the consequences of one's mistakes when one decides to commit to a just and sacred society. Legend has it that in the valley between the Capitoline Hill and the Palatine Hill, Saturn was granted asylum by Janus, Romans later erected the Temple of Saturn at that place, and **Saturnia Tellus** grew, characterized by the Golden Age: a time when men became equal, happy, and prosperous thanks to the mysteries taught to them by the ancient divinity. These mysteries were based on the agricultural and other analogies in mother nature. They have come down to us in the fullness of their esoteric symbolism in Virgil's Bucolics, not just a literary work but a great book of alchemical mysteries. The Asylum of Romulus is said to have stood in what is now Piazza del Campidoglio, on the hill where there was a large oak tree consecrated to the Jupiter Optimus. By establishing this system of asylum, the first king reaffirmed his vision to link this institution to the divine law of Jupiter, tutelary deity of law, hospitality, and aid.

We refer to the study of classical sources, especially to the splendid biography dedicated to him by Plutarch, to know how successfully Romulus conducted his work during his lifetime. Politically, preceding Pythagoras by two centuries, Romulus created and defined the Italic ideal based on the freedom of the individual through land, fire, and blood as opposed to the future Punic model of dependence on the monetary and commercial system. In fact, in the war against Veio, he personally distributed the land to the soldiers and returned the enemy hostages to their families. By this gesture of the king, some senators felt humiliated, but he wanted the purpose of Rome to be an achievement of freedom and not the development of an oligarchic mechanism with large latifundium and exploitation of human beings. As evidence for this principle, we should consider that the Romans transformed the slavery exercised by other ancient peoples in a mechanism of servitude where the slave, through work, could redeem his freedom and become a citizen, educated with the values of the family that had "raised" him in their home.

After thirty-eight years of reign, Romulus ascended into heaven, kidnapped by the whirlwind of a storm while reviewing the troops: this happened in front of all his soldiers. Thus, he was raised to the rank of deity with the name of Quirinus: Rex, Pater Patriae, Filius Martis. He reappeared to his companion Julius Proculus to prove his deification took place. At that time, he entrusted him with the task of transmitting his core message to the people: "Go and announce to the Romans that by practicing temperance and fortitude they'll reach the height of human power." The resurrection of the king was followed by the establishment of Rome. The first king's message was a covenant and was obviously with respect to the **Cultus Deorum Romae**. Rome was blessed with glory as long as it was respected, but when the cult was abandoned, Rome declined. It is a historical fact that every time the rites to the Gods were lightly dusted off, the defenses of Rome invisibly rose with astounding effectiveness. In 408 C.E., Narni escaped the siege of Alaric thanks to the devotion of the city to the ancient Gods. After the public rituals were conducted, a storm broke out and frightened the Goths, who ran away terrified. In the same year, to prevent Alaric from devastating the city, pope Innocentius I permitted the Senate to execute rites to the Gods of Rome, albeit they had to be performed secretly. Not only Alaric accepted a ransom proposed to him by the Romans, but also, he welcomed an ambassadorship of the emperor Honorius. He agreed to return with his Visigoths to the service of Rome as confederates and allies of the Roman army in exchange for money and some hostages. Unfortunately, as good as the Roman rites were, from late antiquity onwards, the same could not be said of men.

Rome is eternal, and its spirit is always ready to re-emerge from the ashes, only if it is a breath of warm love faithful to the pact with Quirinus that awakens it, but every compromise with opposing entities freezes that tender divine heart. Only a Roman with an iron spirit can understand the golden meaning of this. A political intent is not enough to reawaken the fire of Rome, it needs an incorruptible spiritual *vis*, hard and pure as diamond, and we have a history that proves it. To give faith to Rome means to overcome the logic of false reasoning that has besieged the world today, to transcend mysticism, to understand the intrinsic meaning of the value of **Pietas**, and to be able to embody it. Only in this way will the **Foedus** with Quirinus be respected.

So, what is Rome, and why does it charm us even today? Rome is the loving intent to bring justice among men. Rome is immortal because it gives men what their spirits most yearn for: Justice. Cicero, in "The myth of Lupercal in the Bolsena mirror," says, "For all who have preserved their fatherland, furthered it, enriched it, there is in heaven a sure and allotted abode, where they may enjoy an immortality of happiness."

The *Pomerium* and the Walls

Ritually speaking, the story of the birth of Rome handed down to us takes place through a ground furrowing foundation rite, which was performed according to the ancient Latin and Etruscan traditions. This rite involves creating a consecrated orthogonal apportionment of a part of the site followed by the inauguration of a *Pomerium*, near which walls are erected[13]. The *Pomerium* or *Pomoerium* was a sacred boundary around the city of Rome and cities controlled by Rome. In legal terms, Rome existed only within its *Pomerium*, and everything beyond it was simply *Ager*, territory belonging to Rome. According to the tradition, Romulus had traced the line of the *Pomerium* in what had previously been the *Septimontium*, thus inaugurating the new city of Rome. The *Pomerium* was traced based on the auspices, which were interpreted from the flight of birds. In his "Occult philosophy," Cornelius Agrippa explains that the birds flying in the sky transmit the messages of the Gods to earth, and for the Romans, they were, in particular, the messages of Jupiter.

It is interesting to note that the great God is attributed to these priestly arts since he is the father of justice and, therefore, of the law. In fact, Jupiter is derived from the Latin word *Ius*, meaning the law, and the Latin word *Pater*, meaning father. Romulus could identify himself with the unique God of Pythagoras, who proposed the principles and laws that support the universe through conceptual mathematics. The auspice respects certain immutable rules, which were put in place by Jupiter. To respect the will of the God Jupiter, the tracing of the walls was guided by the launch of a javelin anchor carried out immediately after the route suggested by augury. The furrow is drawn with a plow pulled by two oxen and surrounds the area where the javelin fell. The inaugurated *Pomerium* becomes a sacred center. This sacredness is symbolically incorporated into all the elements of the structures that are developed there, and from this sacred center, a new society with noble aims is born.

Bartolomeo Pinelli, Romulus traces the borders of Rome with the plow, 1835.

Image in Public Domain

After the fortification of the Palatine Hill, Romulus offered sacrifices to all the Gods according to the Alban rite and to Hercules according to the ritual established by the mythical sovereign Evander.[14] Evander was the son of Carmenta. It is believed that he met the hero Hercules, greeting him thus, "Hail to you, oh Hercules, son of Jupiter. My mother, a veritable interpreter of the Gods, predicted that you would increase the number of the celestials and that here would be dedicated to you an altar, which the people who will become the most powerful on earth, would call Maximum and using which they would venerate according to your rite."[15] Hercules himself built and consecrated the altar described to him by Evander, which the family of the Potizii maintained as the rite holder until the family had no more descendants. The mystery was then transferred to the public officials. From Titus Livius's passage, we learn that there existed since the beginning of Rome, a mystery cult dedicated to Hercules. Romulus, the mythical hero, represents an initiate into this mystery cult. We, the initiates of today, imitate Romulus, thus attempting to do the great deeds like him.

The city's sacred limit was enlarged over time concomitantly with the extension of the power of Rome. The expansion of the **Pomerium** carried out by the emperor Claudius was explained by some historians as a necessary adaptation to the new conquests of the Romans. To many, it seemed that the expansion of the **Pomerium** represented the extension of the order of Sacred Rome to the wild and barbaric world that surrounded it. Perhaps this is why the Roman Empire lived in the subconscious of the people for hundreds of generations up to the present day because it symbolized and continues to symbolize the reorganization of the forces that are inherent in us, which are capable of perceiving the way of our ancestors who followed the traditional Roman path. Among other reasons, men are attracted to religions because they recognize in the subconscious, but not in the conscious, the initiatory symbolism, and they feel its call. Many have heard the call of the pure soul, in the Penelope of the Odyssey, in the Egyptian Isis, in the Greek Hera, in the Roman Juno, and in the Jewish Myriam but have not consciously recognized it yet.

Beyond the practical benefits, there is something more associated with these walls from the Roman mythology perspective. The myth of the founding fathers, which is a fundamental element of our tradition, preserves within it important esoteric meanings. Rome was founded by the son of the God Mars and the Vestal Virgin Rhea Silvia, who gave birth to the two aspects of reality. As the founder of the city, Romulus represents the pious, sacred, and civil aspects, and Remus, who seeks to overwhelm the city walls, symbolizes the impious, desecrating, and savage aspects. This Remus, therefore, represents the uncultivated nature that surrounds the city, with its forests that contain an untamed fauna, hence its natural, Panic[16], instinctive, and unregulated energy aspects. Tradition tells that Remus, who represents the disorganized instinctive world that seeks, like the Proci of the Odyssey, to take possession of our house, mind, body, or earth, had jumped beyond the new walls, and therefore had been killed by the angered Romulus, the hero who orders the world of man and who, inveighing even with words, added: "so shall die any other man who dares to cross my walls!"

The God Mars is one of the most archaic Italic divinities representing both agriculture and warfare. Warfare is to be understood not as a conquest of others but as a defense of one's territory and people. He is the father of Romulus, who represents the regularization of the countryside. The crops change the sylvan landscape, reordering it as it happens also for the city, distancing the sylvan landscape from Faunus, the chaotic sphere. So, a farm is a regularized transformation of an uncultivated land and similarly the city is a regularized transformation of the countryside. It is a metaphorical victory of the order against chaos, civilization against the wilderness. These walls that delineated the city have not only practical military use but also magical value. They are the protective limits of this sacred circle. Inside the **Pomerium**, one is not allowed to go around with weapons since it represents an ordered and therefore pacified place, where the forces of man no longer clash but move in perfect cosmic harmony. The walls were erected at a certain distance from the **Pomerium** to allow troop movements to defend the city. Finally, the walls have doors, and when magistrates cross through these doors, the crossing imparts auspicious traits to them.

The Square Rome

The foundation of the city includes a precise layout of roads that goes beyond physical engineering and incorporates esoteric metaphysical designs. A detailed discussion on this subject would require several separate publications, but we touch upon a few concepts in this work. The reader is encouraged to explore these and other esoteric designs of our ancestors under the guidance of an experienced teacher. ***Via Sacra***[17] was the first such design in ancient Rome. It was the main artery of the city. Its western end was at the top of the Capitoline hill, where there was a majestic temple of Jupiter called ***Iovis Optimi Maximi Capitolini***, and its eastern end was at what now are the ruins of the ***Amphitheatrum Flavium*** or the Colosseum. It ran through the ***Forum Romanum***, the religious, cultural, commercial, and political center of ancient Rome. Along that path were some of the most important religious sites of the ***Forum Romanum***. The streets that ran east-west were called ***Decamanus***, and the north-south ones were called ***Cardo***, and the intersection was called ***Compitum***. Each administrative district or ***Vici*** at its principal ***Compita*** had a shrine for the district's guardian deities, the ***Lares Compitales***. The ***Via Sacra*** as the principal ***Decaman*** of Rome had them as well at all its principal ***Compita***. One cannot say exactly who these were as they changed from time to time, but one thing was for certain though, there always were a pair of them, one masculine and the other feminine. Every intersection represented the joining of these two forces, with the east-west ***Decamanus*** representing the feminine and the north-south ***Cardo*** representing the masculine.

Another esoteric metaphysical design incorporated into the city was the connection between the macrocosm and the microcosm. The universe was understood as the macrocosm and the man as the macrocosmic universe's microcosmic projection. Thus, the ***Via Sacra*** can be understood as the microcosmic projection of the sky with the seven major celestial objects of Roman astrology and astronomy. The temple of Jupiter and the temple of Saturn are easily identifiable even today from their ruins and can be symbolically associated with the

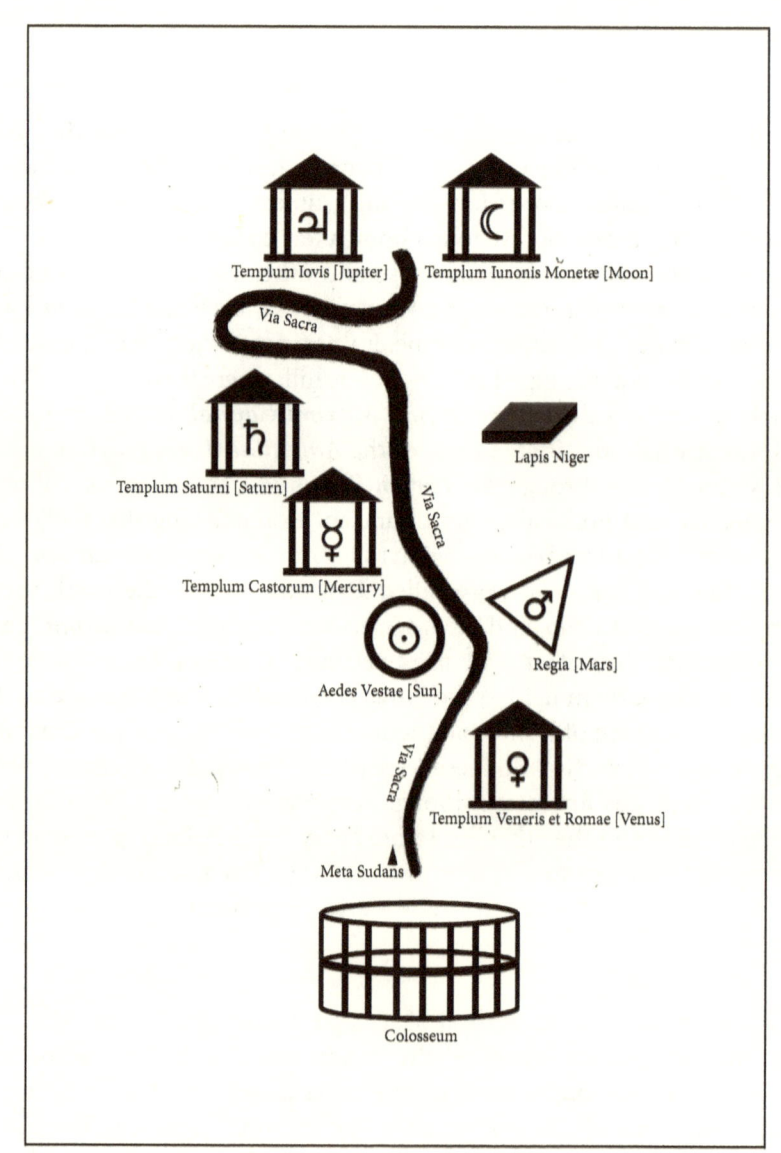

Temples along Via Sacra's sinuous route from Capitoline Hill to Coliseum are understood as microcosmic projections of the seven major celestial planets.

planets that have their names. Esoteric analysis that shows the elements of the remaining five celestials, Mercury, Venus, Mars, Moon, and the Sun, is a subject matter of a more detailed work to be published later.

Janus is the God of beginnings, gates, transitions, time, duality, doorways, passages, and endings. He is usually depicted as having two faces. The Temple of Janus stood in the Roman Forum near the Basilica Aemilia, along the Argiletum. These temple doors were known as the "Gates of Janus" and were closed in times of peace and opened in times of war. This is because, besides being the guardian of the threshold for the invisible world, Janus is also the God of war and peace[18]. Janus presided over war and peace according to whether he appeared as Patulcius or as Clusius[19]. The two thresholds of *Via Sacra* were marked by the doors of Janus Curiatius - Iuno Sororia to the east and Janus Quirinus - Cloacina to the west. The western entrance to the *Via Sacra*, near the Velabrum where the Janus Geminus / Quirinus[20] shrine was located, is considered by many scholars as that from which the armies passed when they left for the war, whose season began in March. The eastern entrance of *Via Sacra* was instead reserved for the return from the battle[21], and fighters passed through it to purify themselves from the massacres done. Beyond war and peace, Janus is the guardian of all physical doors, which lead into a sacred space, including the doors in the **Pomerium** that allow the passage between the sylvan and the urban. On an esoteric level, we can understand that the lord of the gates beyond the physical aspects provides a path to higher spiritual conditions in an individual. When Janus opens the doors within the individual, he sparks a realization, and when he closes these internal doors, one loses connection to this inner divine. So esoterically, Janus presides over the war that the man faces against himself and similarly presides over peace once it is reached when the individual has finally realized himself.

The esoteric dual aspect of things is structurally incorporated in the topography of the republican city of Rome. In front of the place where rallies were held, the heart of the Roman forum from where the *Via Sacra* starts, there is an esoteric sequence consisting of the three temples dedicated to Saturn, the Castores, and Vesta, respectively. Under the stretch of the road connecting the sequence, there exists a **lapis niger**[22]. Saturn and

Vesta represent two opposite esoteric aspects, but they are joined together by the Castores. Saturn represents the material world, wealth, and earth. The Goddess Vesta represents the opposite end of this esoteric duality and is the guardian of the sacred fire; she represents the divinity of the Logos. Saturn and Vesta's duality enshrined in the structures of ancient temples of Rome symbolically represents the duality that exists everywhere, including within ourselves. Even though both Saturn and Vesta coexist everywhere in mother nature, one aspect prevails over the other and vice versa. The divine twins, the Castores, whose shrine is situated between those of Saturn and Vesta, connects the two, the material and the divine. On an esoteric level, the Castores symbolically represent the effort that is needed to harmonize this duality. It is up to men to do the sacred rituals and work to balance these two powerful forces for their own benefit. Romulus is the hero who managed to do this. He established the needed order between the sacred divine things and the voluptuous material things by inaugurating a city within himself first through the rite of the inauguration of the square Rome.

This balance is well expressed in the Roman ritual calendar. There are days dedicated to the superior Gods, which involve the raising of divine forces of the human spirit. Then there are days consecrated to the sylvan deities such as Faunus or the infernal ones such as Consu[23] or Vediovis, which draw men's material and animal instincts. In the Roman tradition, there is another similar esoteric concept. According to this concept, the human being consists of four bodies. They are the physical body, the soul, the intelligence, and the spirit. On an elemental level, they correspond to earth, water, air, and fire, and on a macrocosmic level to Saturn, Moon, Mercury, and the Sun. The Roman patrician, observing the ritual calendar and thereby balancing the Saturn and Vesta in himself, can thus become a hero like his first sovereign, by being able to reorder the four forces that live within himself[24]. Then the squaring of the circle takes place, that is, the reorganization of the four elements, each of which are linked to the aforementioned four forces that make up the man, the foundation of the square Rome on the circle of the Palatine hill.

The Doors

The gates we are referring to now are not the nine gates of Plotinus, but those erected in the proto-urban settlement of Rome and the first urban phase of the city. The esoteric meaning hidden in these structures is fascinating. Carandini defines the doors found on the Palatine as an emblem of the Cosmogony and Hierogamy of the Latins.[25] The door, when understood in its practical function as a passage, is called **Iugum**. Physically though, a door consists of four elements, the architrave, the two plummers, and the threshold. To these physical elements correspond certain traditional Roman deities, defined by some as demons[26], or as **Geni**. The architrave's deity is Stercutus, the God of garbage and purification. A broom is considered a symbol of this deity. When any city, palace, temple, house, or any other living place is purified, the garbage is swept out the door. The architrave is also referred to with the feminine term, namely Pila. Pila is the counterpart of the plummer, which is also called Pilum. Pilum refers to the left and the right jambs that hold the door to the wall, and the corresponding deities of these two elements are the Picumnus and Pilumnus. A pestle was considered Pilum's symbol. The Pilum also represent the spear, a symbol of the God Mars, who also happens to be the God of fertility. So, Pila indicates the female horizontal elements and the Pilum the male vertical ones. The fourth element, the threshold, constitutes the border of the house with the external, hostile world associated with the infernal demon Faunus[27]. At the same time, the threshold corresponds to the God Limentinus and Mana, the mother of the Gods accompanying the dead.[28]

Picumnus and Pilumnus, together with Stercutus, are the guardians of the spaces that are accessed through the corresponding doors, and in this role, they prevent infernal forces that live beyond the doors from passing through. This protection from harmful forces is particularly provided to the woman of the house when she is in labor and about to deliver a child. Varro and Augustine of Hippo hand down a ritual for this life event. When a woman gives birth to a child, she and the newly born child are susceptible to the attack from the chaotic and wild world outside. So, our ancestors

Temple of the Divo Romulo, Rome.

conducted a ritual to prevent Faunus from harming them in any way. On the first night after the child's birth, Picumnus, Pilumnus, and Stercutus were summoned as superior deities[29] and were symbolically associated with three men who conducted this ritual. Two of the three men represented Picumnus and Pilumnus. Of these two, one wielded an ax and the other a lance or a pestle, and they ritually hit the wooden threshold of the door and in the process produced wooden shavings from it. The third man, who represents Stercutus, swept away these threshold shavings with a broom.[30] Thus, Picumnus and Pilumnus, under the protection of Stercutus, drove out the external intruder Faunus. This ritual is a unique characteristic of the Roman tradition. We see here the incarnation of the deities in the executives of the rite, who use the tools attributed to these deities to perform their function.

The Palace

The first royal palaces were most likely situated on the northern slope of the Palatine because North is the direction of God Jupiter. From the time of Romulus, the sovereign held all the major powers. So, he was also a **Rex Sacrorum** and a **Pontifex Maximus**. In fact, inside the palace, there was a shrine, where the sacred objects revered in the imagination of the Romans were kept. Among these, there were Hastae Martiae, the famous spear of the God Mars falling from the sky, and Ancilia, his shield. The palace also preserved within it the Lituus with which the hero drew the wishes for the city's foundation. Around 600 B.C.E., in the royal age, the shrine was separated from the sovereign's residence, and the office of **Rex Sacrorum** was created. So, the concept of separation of powers was already in place before the foundation of the Roman Republic. Tarquinius Superbus was the seventh king of Rome, and his house was built outside the sacred area, as well as the building that housed the Mars and Ops shrines, which were separated from the sovereign's palace, probably by Tarquinius Priscus[31], the first ruler of the Etruscan dynasty.

The prominence of these two deities shows the balanced thought of the ancient Romans. Mars is not only a God of war but is also the agricultural guardian. He makes the fields bloom, grows crops abundantly, and multiplies the generative energy. When the season of Mars begins in spring, nature is in its nascent state. Persephone leaves the underworld, and with her emergence, the flowers blossom, and the fruits ripen in abundance until the summer. Autumn and winter mark the cyclical decline of this generative energy, which our ancestors associated with Mars. With the end of summer, Mars becomes weak, and Persephone is buried in the underworld. During this time, without the efforts of man, the earth would not bear the fruits expected in the following spring. For this reason, man must now rest in order to be available to rejuvenate after the winter. The Roman man must stop the war activities to devote himself to the care of the earth. Now it is the time of Goddess Ops. She is the divinity of the pantries of the house, a female deity, according to some scholars, linked to the role of the woman who takes care of domestic affairs.[32] She is therefore concerned with the safekeeping and management of the harvest, protecting the martial energy that has fertilized the earth by ensuring that the food accumulated is enough for the autumn and winter. As it is always in the Roman tradition, we have a pair of deities here too that preside over everyday functions and represent the balanced collaboration in the Roman family. The man engages in the harvest and the war while the woman manages the food supply and the domestic affairs. At the same time, since Mars is a symbol of virile energy, his human counterpart, the man, must sow the woman, who is the earthly counterpart of Ops. Hence, the woman must be fertile to use the man's virility and have children, who are essential for continuing the Roman society and its traditions.

Lasha Tskhondia, A derivative work of a 3D model - L.VII.C

Lasha Tskhondia, CC BY-SA 3.0 <https://creativecommons.org/licenses/by-sa/3.0>, via Wikimedia Commons

The Temple of Vesta

The temple of Vesta was probably the most important institution in ancient Rome. It is where the sacred fire of the Romans was kept. Unlike other temples dedicated to various Gods and Goddesses where their respective idols were the temple's central element, in the Temple of Vesta, the fire was the idol. Daughter of Saturn and Rhea, sister of Jupiter and Juno, the eternal virgin Goddess Vesta is the hearth's sacred guardian. Fire represents life, and the round temple in which fire stood represented the world. Even in the heavens on Mount Olympus, where the Gods reside, her abode is right in the center of all the other Gods. In February, the full moon is sacred to Vesta, and the festival of Vestalia in June is dedicated to her.

Her famous temple in Rome along the ***Via Sacra*** was built by Numa Pompilius, the second king of Rome. He lived in the Sabine Curi and was as comprehensively educated in both the sacral and common affairs as was possible at that time. In addition to the Temple of Vesta and the associated Vestal institutions, Numa Pompilius established many important religious and political frameworks of Rome. These include the Roman Calendar, the cult of Mars, the cult of Jupiter, the cult of Romulus, and the office of **Pontifex Maximus**. According to the opinion of Livius, Numa had to be by his natural predisposition a tempered spirit of virtue. In it, he was instructed not so much by "foreign" doctrines as by the rigid and severe discipline of the Sabines, a people as righteous as it gets. To ensure the continuous favor of the Gods, he created different priestly colleges so that Rome does not become negligent in conducting the rituals and ceremonies of the tradition. He also instituted the Vestal Virgins, native Alba's priesthood with the same lineage as the founder, Numa Pompilius himself. To these virgin priestesses, so that they could be diligent custodians of the temple, he assigned a state salary. By the vow of chastity and other privileges, the priestesses became venerable[33].

These Vestal Virgins who maintained the temple were women from the royal families of Rome. They swore an oath to celibacy while they were in that role. Some of them remained virgins lifelong and served the temple, and others married after they spent several years of their life at the temple. They were symbolically wives of the **Pontifex Maximus** and had a powerful position in Roman society. Our ancestors believed that, as long as the sacred temple fire of Rome was tended by the Vestals, the city will maintain its ideal function in the world, but if it were extinguished, Rome would lose its purpose. The Vestals, therefore, had the arduous task of keeping the flame and through it Rome's exalted position always alive. If we study history carefully, we will realize that our ancestors were right. The decline of the great Roman empire can be traced to the destruction of the temple of Vesta and its vestal institutions. Our ancestors understood the importance of sacred fire, the temple, its vestal institutions, and its rituals. For this reason, the careless Vestal who let the sacred flame go extinct was punished atrociously.

The Vestal can be coveted by the Roman Lare, and in her womb, she keeps the twins, who are the two aspects of all things. The first is the pious, sacred, and orderly Romulus Rex Romae, while the other is the profane, violent, and aggressive Remus. It is necessary but not sufficient to have a physical temple of Vesta. On a spiritual level, the temple of Vesta must also be established within us. The virgin and immaculate soul must look after the sacred fire to give life to the sublime idea of personal understanding and realization. Esoterically speaking, this is the meaning of the temple and the myth of Vesta. As long as our ancestors had both the physical temple of Vesta in their city and the spiritual temple of the sacred fire in their consciousness, Rome was a great nation-state. H. C. Agrippa, in chapter 5 of volume 1 of his work, "Three Books of Occult Philosophy or Magic," succinctly explains the nature of fire and gives us an insight into our ancestors thought on this sacred subject. An extract of the same has been reproduced in Appendix 4 of the book.

Capitulum III
De Pietate et religione

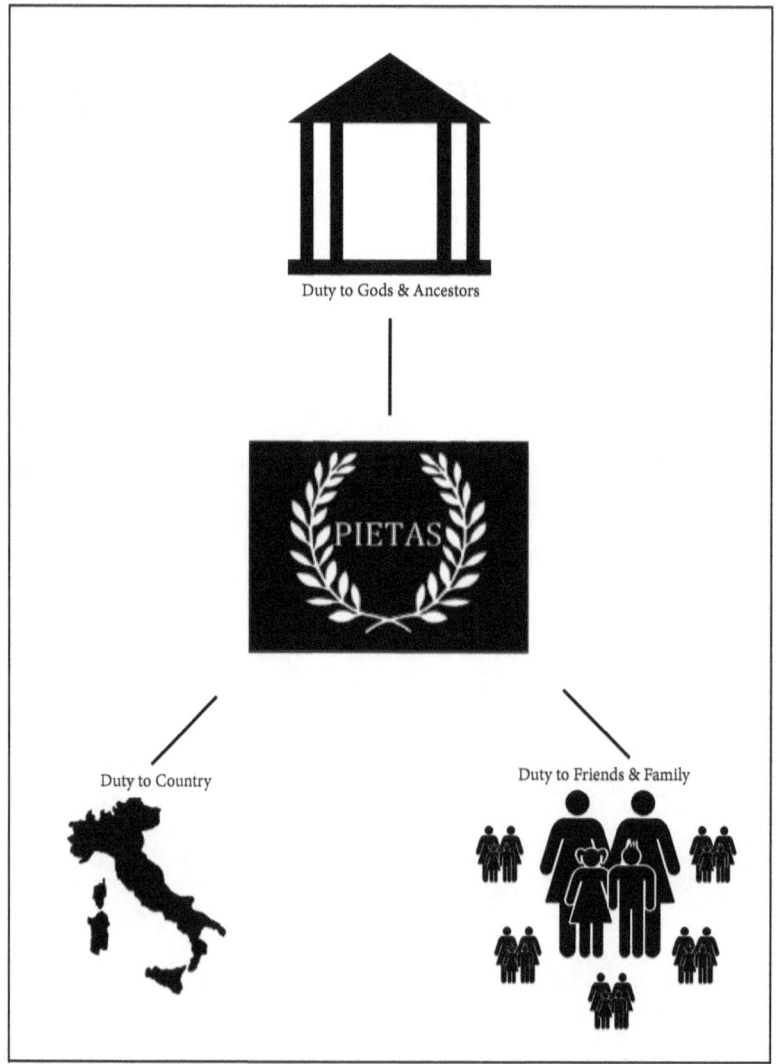

Pietas is not religion but a sacred duty to the Gods, the ancestors, the country, family, and friends.

Randomhero, Italy Map.

Randomhero, CC BY-SA 3.0 <https://creativecommons.org/licenses/by/3.0/us/legalcode>, via The Noun Project.

Flaticon.com, Family Icon. - This icon is from Flaticon.com.

Understanding *Pietas*

The Roman Tradition makes a clear distinction between **Pietas** and **religio**. Understanding these two aspects for a Roman is quite different compared to the common understanding of the two words piety and religion. The Roman word **Pietas** means deep respect for tradition and the rules of sacred law, which establish peace between humans and deities. One who respects the sacred days of the Roman calendar and diligently conducts the required rituals in accordance with the ancient rules is pious. On the other hand, those who carry out a massacre, when this is not prescribed just to please the Gods, are tainted with religiosity and are considered impious, in the same way as those who do not comply with the dictates prescribed by the sacred law. [34] It is important for us to understand that the Roman sees the religious as superstitious. The ancients knew very well that divinities are nothing more than projections that arise from ourselves. In contrast, the religious see them detached from us, imagining them only in their anthropomorphic form, thus ignoring their true essence. It is certainly difficult to say how many enlightened people there might have been in Rome, but we can say for sure that every **Pietas** person had the opportunity to achieve enlightenment by following the rules and conducting the rituals as per the sacred calendar.

The pious man is moderate, and this moderation is evident in the way he spends his resources and time. He divides his life between family, work, piety, and civic activity. There is a very intimate corner in the house, where the **Pater Familias** performs the ritual duties assigned to him, respecting the rules of the noble cult to which he belongs. In this sacred area is placed the **Lararium**, which is the small domestic replica of the temple, inside which are placed the images and the figurines of the ancestors and the Gods honored by the family, the Lares and the **Penates**. In addition, in this corner, a tripod or brazier is usually placed to light the fire for offerings to the Gods that manifest themselves and communicate with men through its flame. The ritual is performed in the morning when the Sun or conscience rises in the sky. The ritual opens with a dedication to Janus, the prayer then continues to the spirit, Genius Loci of the place or of the house, often the Lares and the ancestors. Then the prescribed ritual is performed, not forgetting the salutation to the Gens deity and to the own Genius. The closure can be preceded by a piacular formula that allows not to be guilty in the event of accidental errors during the ceremony. As an example, let us try to imagine how to perform the ritual of the Potizii's **Pater Familias**, holders of the cult of Hercules, in a day dedicated to the deified hero. After the ablutions, secluded in front of his **Lararium**, a previously purified environment, at the hour when the Sun rises, a **Primus Potitius** would recite the following orations facing north after burning a grain of frankincense.

Opening - SALVE JANE, SACRAE PORTAE DOMINE, ADMITTE ME CORAM NUMINA LUCENTIA.

To the Genius Loci - SALVE MARS, GENIE LOCI, TIBI OFFERO HOC THUS ET TU SIES MIHI PROPITIUS. ITA EST.

Then to the Gens deity - SALVE HERCULES, DIVUS INCOMMENSURABILIS ROBORI, TIBI OFFERO HOC THUS ET TU MIHI PROPITIUS SIES ET INDICA MIHI VIAM SCENTIAE PERFECTAE, ITA EST.

Do not forget the Genius - HIC ET NUNC UBICUMQUE ET SEMPER PRISTINUS GENIUS, MEUS PRAEEST IN ME, SUB SPECIE MERCURII. SALVE ALBIANUS, TIBI OFFERO HOC THUS ET TU SIES MIHI PROPITIUS. ITA EST.

Closing- QUOD BONUM FAUSTUMQUE SIT. ITA EST. ILLICET

Let us now understand this rite in a bit more detail. It opens with a request for the consent of the God Janus, who presides at the door for all human endeavors.[35] The ancient Janus, the two-faced God who causes man to come out of the chaos of material life and to enter the ritual in harmony with the Gods so that the ritual performer's entreaties can be heard by the Gods. Just as divinity is present within us, it is also present in the place, and it is a form of energy of Nature with a specific function. So, next for successful completion of the ceremony with unobstructed communication with the Gods, the Genius Loci, the divinity in charge of the place where the rite is being performed is sought. In this example, we have shown that **Primus Potitius** is performing the ritual in a place sacred to Mars. So, the Genius Loci in this case is the God Mars. If, however, the divinity of a place is not known, Cicero says to turn to this formula *quisquis es sive quo alio nomine fas est appellari, sive mas sive femina*, which in English means "whoever you are or with any other name you get called, either male or female." The divinity of the place could also be an elementary spirit like an elf, a gnome, a dwarf, or a nymph. A supplication to these entities is also necessary so that no astral beings appear and disrupt the ceremony by breaking apart our communication with the divinity we are trying to evoke and to secure the first good wishes. The oration to the Genius of one's own Gens is performed only after the oration in honor to Janus and the Genius Loci. To perform a perfect ritual and to expect a good outcome from it, the practitioners needed to evoke their personal Genius as well, who presides over personal development. Having done this, there will not be any opposition from the personal Genius to any kind of what we call "psychic light phenomena." This kind of phenomena arises from practicing the mysteries of Hercules. Initiates are the only ones who know their Genius and thus they can ask them to be propitious, in exchange of a grain of frankincense or any other kind of offer they prefer. This means one has to be an initiate that has gone through the mysteries of Hercules to perform this ritual. Finally, to reconfirm the will of divine consent, the rite is closed with the said formula "may it be good and fortunate. So it is." **Ita Est**, unlike the Christian, "so it be," is not a hope for good wishes, but the certainty of having worked in the right and having followed the dictates of **Pietas**.

Certainly, the pious man not only understands the rules of sacred law but also puts them into action even before understanding them. This ability to understand the rules over time by practicing them is what constitutes personal development. So, performing the ritual as per the mandated rules, even without understanding its hermetic meanings, and gaining that esoteric understanding through ritual, is **Pietas**, but changing the ritual based on mystical feelings or personal interpretation is **religio**, which is considered superstition. **Pietas** is therefore scientific practice of ritual whereas **religio** is superstition born out of anxiety and fear. The latin word **religio** comes from the combination of root "re-," which means again, and "Lego," which means to bind. But what gets bound? The myth binds symbols that metaphorically represent the truth. Myth and the ritual are like lock and key. Myth veils the truth inside the symbol and the ritual unveils it. This veiling and unveiling process is essential because the truth cannot be communicated but must be conquered through experience. Religion by superimposing additional binds and removing the ritual, locks the path to experiential truth and leads to dogma driven superstition. According to ancient Romans, religion was healthy as long as it maintained the values of **Pietas**. When they abandoned it, there arose superstitio, which was morally condemned by them. The law of **Pietas** is understood only when one enters into harmony by purifying oneself from everything, not only from physical impurities but also from impressions absorbed on the lunar body, such as religious convictions, which bind us to our Rational conscience, preventing us from reaching into our hearts, where Ancus Marcius would give us the gift of understanding it. The priests of our traditional system assigned to our Gentile ancestors the rituals to be practiced along with all the related rules and procedures, and if they practiced these rituals according to these dictates piously, they reached the purification of the soul and were then able to reach different levels of awareness and understanding of things. So, it was the sincere performance of the prescribed rituals that led to the awareness. Obviously, these practices could be sustained only by respecting all the rules of the sacred law, such as abstaining from Venus on certain days and following a prescribed diet, as taught by Macrobius in his work the "Saturnalia."

The Temple

The Roman temple is a place of contact between the human and the divine. It is a square, a geometric form derived from the idea, espoused by the Pythagoreans as well, of reorganizing the four elements of Nature. Each side of the square indicates a distinct element of Nature, and the space within it is permeated by the remaining fifth element,[36] which is the essence that allows contact between the human and divine world. It is for this reason that the temple on earth was used by the Haruspex for performing the auguries, the process by which the divine messages of the Gods were interpreted based on the flight of the birds. At the University of Rome "La Sapienza," the archaeologist Andrea Carandini, as well as the epigraphist Silvio Panciera, have carried out some studies on these ancient practices. Thanks to these sources, we now know the way of the omens, but the interpretation methods were not known until a temple with an Auguraculum was excavated with nine stones, one in the center indicating the Sun and eight other delimiters indicating the main cardinal points. In Andrea Carandini's exhibition on the foundation of Rome, which took place in 2000 C.E. at the Baths of Diocletian, the example of an augural temple was reconstructed, and auspices were enacted according to the ancient texts. The temple on earth corresponds to an analogous temple in the heavens. The one in the heavens is the reflection of the earthly one, and it is the portion of the heavens in which the divine signs are manifested, and these signs are then interpreted by an augur. The auspices were consulted by the magistrates before taking any important decision, and every time they passed the line of the **Pomerium**, the boundary between the **Imperium Domi** and the **Imperium Maius**. So, before embarking on military campaigns or carrying out political functions in the city. Similarly, the Sibylline books, which were a collection of oracular utterances, were consulted at other times.

In his monumental work on the history of Rome, Titus Livius, "Ab Urbe Condita," tells us that Numa Pompilius, the second king of Rome before assuming the post of the king, had the auspices by means of an augur drawn for him. His description provides interesting insights into this practice. We provide here a translated version of the same.

Upon being chosen to lead Rome, Numa Pompilius wanted that the Gods should be consulted for him just as his predecessor, Romulus, in founding the city had drawn the auspices before taking over the kingdom. An augur was then summoned, and he led Numa to a rock. There they both sat on a stone, facing the south. The augur sat on his left, with his head veiled, and he held in his right hand a lituus, a hooked stick with no knots. Then, as they embraced the city and the countryside with their eyes and invoked the Gods, the augur marked the space from east to west and proclaimed the parts toward noon fortunate, the ones toward the north unfortunate, mentally determining before him a point, the farther to which the eyes could reach. Then the augur passed the lituus into his left hand and set his right hand on Numa's head and prayed:

Iuppiter Pater, si est fas hunc Numam Pompilium, cuius ego caput teneo, regem Romae esse, uti tu signa nobis certa adclarassis inter eos fines, quos feci. Jupiter Father, if it is a divine decree that this Numa Pompilius, of whom I touch the head, be king of Rome, manifest to us sure signs among those limits that I have traced.

Then the augur announced the auspices he wished to receive and availed them. Numa then descended from that auspicious place, having received the divine signs, and proclaimed the king.[37]

This augury of Numa exemplifies the function of the temple on earth and the temple in Coelo, in whose limits the Gods are invoked to communicate with the humans. Divination is, however, not the only purpose for a temple. The temple can be used in other ways for any other ritual by any priest. To the profane, it is forbidden to enter the inaugurated squares or the temples because, with their impurities, they could contaminate it and thus lead to a loss of its magical function. Between the architectural temple and the augural temple consisting of a simple enclosed square, there is no difference, except that the architectural temple is always on a raised

Guillaume Rouille, Numa Pompilus.

Guillaume Rouille, Public domain, via Wikimedia Commons.

podium, and therefore due to the presence of the walls, it is not possible to sit and turn around to look on the horizon to be able to draw the auspices. In the architectural temples, however, the interpretation of divine consent takes place in other ways. For example, the haruspices were able to read the future through the entrails of the animals sacrificed for ritual banquets. We will return to this sacred art later. A temple is, therefore, a physical place of contact with the Supere -superior and Infere -inferior dimensions. The temples dedicated to Hades were located close to caves or in semi-hypogean environments. This should not be surprising. Our observation should not stop on the simple and superstitious conviction of contact with the entities that inhabit the interior of the earth or the underworld. These places do not exist in our external reality, but in a secret world difficult to perceive and penetrate, this dimension is closer to us than we can think. Ulysses easily finds a door through which to go to the underworld to sacrifice a black ram. In addition to physical structures, created in places where Gods have manifested their favors, there is a creature in Nature capable of penetrating this secret world. This creature is permeated by the active divine essence more than our mind or dreams can imagine. It is the meeting point between the pan and the divine stars, which are higher and farthest from our planet and invisible even to our telescopes. The creature has within itself the potentiality of the divine par excellence. That creature is the human being. With his ability to adapt and change the surrounding Nature according to his needs, the human being has been considered by the ancients as the perfect creature. He is the excellent creation of the Olympic Gods and has the potential to attain their divinity. And it is from the man, says Vitruvius in his De Architectura, that the Doric order bases its proportions, as well as the most graceful, slender, and delicate Ionic order bases its proportions on the size of the woman.[38] Our ancestors wanted to build the temples as perfect places for the perfect Gods. So, they found the inspiration for building what was sacred looking at Mother Nature because Nature is the physical reflection of divine perfection. In other words, Nature is the reflection of the divine around us.

In addition to the priests, the senators, who were free to hold meetings and make decisions in the presence of the deities, could also enter the Roman temples. A council of war would easily be held in the temple of Mars since the expert par excellence in this field would rightly inspire those who had gathered in his temple. For example, when Cicero had to defend the Rhodians, who, despite their loyalty to Rome, risked losing their freedom, he decided to convene the Senate in the temple of Jupiter Stator. This is the temple that Romulus built following a vow he made for its erection during the mythical battle held in the city against the Sabines, a battle in which the Romans did not back away but kept their position with pride and faith. In the same way, the Rhodians remained faithful to Rome and asked the famous orator to take up the defense of their cause. So, in that temple of Jupiter that Romulus had built after prevailing over the Sabines, Cicero convinced the Roman Senators about the Rhodian cause with the famous Oratio pro Rohdiensibus. As already mentioned, the temple is founded and dedicated to a deity in the place where the deity was manifested, either by the epiphanic appearance of the deity or by favor of the deity manifesting its will through the request of a devout practitioner of that deity's ritual worship. At other times the temples are founded for the necessity of having a place of contact with the higher dimensions. The latter are well described in Cicero's Somnium Scipionis. First, when it was decided to erect a Roman temple, an augur had to exorcise the place from any kind of impurity and then trace and consecrate the square where the cell would later be built. The architectural work was therefore carried out, always according to the esoteric criteria, so that the sacred place would bear sacred symbols. The temple could be dedicated to one or more deities, and for this, the appropriate rituals were conducted by specially appointed priests. The foundation ritual and organization of the temple was decided by the Pontifex, holder of the rules and laws of the sacred.

Esoterism and Exoterism

Every religion has both an esoteric and an exoteric side. Esoteric is the actual substance, while the exoteric is the shape, the external, the symbol without its hidden meaning. For example, the Cornucopia exoterically speaking is a horn full of fruits, flowers and etcetera, while esoterically it represents abundance.

The term esoterism is of Greek origin and is well explained by Plato, who opposes it to exoterism. The word hermeticism is the closest synonym to the meaning that Socrates wanted to attribute to esotericism. This consists in the real interpretation of the symbols, often manifested in public rituals, as in the processions of the Dionysia[39] or in the Eleusinian ones, and these symbols are always present in various myths. The Greek philosopher is very self-aware when she says that myths are not for everyone. A layperson or a fervent Christian would say that mythology is only for children and, as many historians of the religions have written in a biased way, that it is only the product of primitive and superstitious minds. Certainly, we are all in agreement that only primitive minds have conceived social systems like Greek Democracy and the Roman Republic! Certainly, we all agree in considering primitives, the civilizations that have managed to bring water into the desert,[40] when even today humanity is unable to solve the perennial drought in some places! Roman law is the basis of modern law. Ancient philosophy was the first true rational research that man has ever faced on the things that surround and permeate him, and there are those who dare to say that our ancestors were primitive.

The philosophy of the ancients is not simplistic as it is accused to be since what the Greeks say, that man is made up of four basic elements, is pure truth. We are made of "earth," which is our physical body. We are made of "water," which is our soul. Just as fluids occupy the vessels into which they are poured, so the soul occupies the receptacle of our physical body. We are made of "air," which is our intelligence, and it is even more impalpable than the soul. Finally, we are made of "fire," which is our spirit.

De Pietate et Religione | 45

The temple's form is derived from the idea of reorganizing the four elements of nature. Each side of the temple indicates a distinct element of nature, and the space within it is permeated by the remaining fifth element, which is the essence that allows contact between the human and divine world. Likewise, the man is made up of the same four basic elements, earth is his body, air is his mind, water is his soul and fire is his spirit.

The spirit manifests itself in us through heat. I speak about this from personal experience and not based on cultural beliefs, and so you can also independently verify the existence of these bodies within you. You can do this by performing prayers at the right times, abstaining from food and Venus when necessary, maintaining an external and internal balance, which will lead to the moment when the consciousness of subtle bodies will awaken, and you can confirm to yourself that the ancient knowledge of our ancestors across the Mediterranean was permeated with the truth. Unfortunately, this great knowledge was then misrepresented by those who preferred the creation of servile religions in order to establish their power on the masses and control them. What a shame! Men, free yourselves! Do not remain trapped in the exoteric meaning of things, which have been marketed by the promoters of the servile religions. The hermetic mystery is that each symbol has a double meaning. There is an exoteric one for those who have not been initiated and an esoteric one, which is addressed to those who are initiated into the mysteries. Let us take some trivial examples. Romulus exoterically represents the good and the justice in the universal dualism, and esoterically represents the pious, sacred, and civil aspects of ourselves. Thus, Penelope exoterically represents conjugal fidelity, but in the hermetic reality of things, that is esoterically speaking, she is the pure soul that the initiated hero must rediscover and embrace, but before that, he must face a series of trials. Likewise, Odysseus' journey represents the search for truth on the part of man, but esoterically the Odyssey, the sacred book of Greek culture (later also adopted by the Latins for its wisdom), represents a series of rituals and evidence that the initiate (hero) must face to be able to realize the first part of the work. Today, there are esoteric currents that spread truth for hidden symbols. Therefore, it is necessary to always go beyond the symbol, to penetrate the esoteric truth of things, perceptible only in the world of ideas.

The Art of Haruspex

Among the most practiced Roman divinatory arts, we find the augural and haruspical ones. We talked about augury earlier in this book, and here we will discuss haruspicy. If we go back two thousand years, reading the pages of Homer, Cato, and many others, we discover that the Greek and Roman Gods liked the hecatomb of bulls and lambs. On the most important feast days, our ancestors performed a ritual sacrifice of a pig, a lamb, and a bull. While they considered the flesh in a negative sense because it was devoid of the spirit of life, they sublimated that negativity with the sacred sacrifice. They offered the animals to the chosen Gods holding the banquet in their honor, and the sacrifice was the medium through which they entered into communion with the Gods. The haruspicy was practiced as a part of this ritual sacrifice. In exchange for the sacrificial offerings given to them, the Gods sent through the entrails of the victims certain messages to the men giving them insight into the past, present, and future. These insights helped our Romans ancestors undertake prophylactic initiatives and avoid erroneous actions. The hecatombs were public rituals undertaken by the city or state and were elaborate affairs conducted for public welfare. Sometimes priests assisted even private citizens to offer these sacrifices to the Gods to help them with their personal questions. So, the haruspices sacrificed the victims and then read the entrails to find answers to the questions posed as per the request of the citizen. This sacred science was practiced not only in Greece and Rome but also in Mesopotamia, and it is believed that the Romans had learned it from the Etruscans. Even today, in some inland areas of Calabria, there are people who know how to interpret certain omens to predict the future, with extreme precision, from the organs of pigs that they kill in December.

This divine art was treated no different than any other sacred knowledge and was passed from the teacher to selected students, who spent many years of their life studying and perfecting this art. It was a well-established science with theory, models, and practice. Older priests taught the younger ones how to read the bowels on models of prepared

48 | De Pietate et Religione

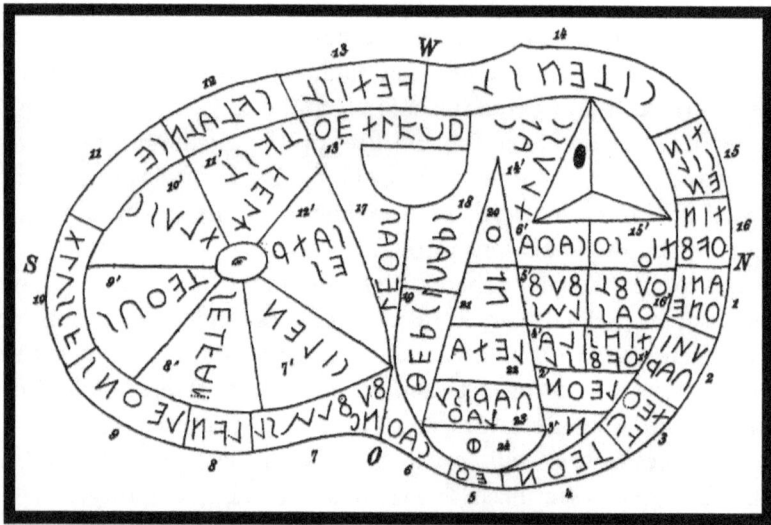

Wilhelm Deecke, Diagram of the bronze liver of Piacenza.

Wilhelm Deecke (1831–1897), Public domain, via Wikimedia Commons.

organs. While in augury, the sky and the flight of the birds formed the basis of the interpretation, in haruspicy, it was the liver. There is a model of a well-preserved bronze liver in the Museum of Etruscology of Villa Giulia in Rome. Also, in the museum of Baghdad, we can see the terracotta models that were used by the Chaldean priests. These Chaldean models are very similar to the Roman ones. The liver was divided into regions and each region corresponded to a divinity. The various minute features of the liver, such as lines, colors, and protuberances of the liver, were interpreted to forecast the future. The location of the sign within the liver's geography decided whether it was a propitious or an ominous prediction.

Sacerdotal Colleges

In Rome, all the priests belonged to public colleges and were maintained by the state. They performed the tasks dictated by the **Pontifex Maximus**. The city's tribunal councils voted the members of the major colleges, which dealt with the management and production of sacred law. The first was the pontifical colleges, whose membership consisted of 20 **viri clarissimi**, who were members of the senatorial **ordo**, 16 **Pontifices**, the **Rex Sacrorum**, and three major **Flamines**, those of Jupiter, Mars, and Quirinus. Another 19 were cavaliers/knights[41]. Three were invested with the minor pontificate, 10 of the minor flaminates were related to the other important divinities, and 6 were vestals, who were chosen by the **Pontifex Maximus**. There were three other major colleges. There was one for the augury, which designed the temples and drew wishes for the exercise of public, private, or sacred functions. Then there was that of the **quindecemviri sacris faciundi**,[42] which had 19 members who were charged with the task of administering the sacred law of the cults of the Greek rite and consulting the Sibillini books for the Senate. Finally, the last of the major colleges was that of the **septemviri epulonum**, that is, the seven men assigned to the sacred banquets. They were responsible for celebrating public banquets and processions on the occasion of the great games held during the prescribed ritual days.

In addition to the major colleges, there were a few minor colleges as well. The members of the minor colleges were chosen by cooptation from the major ones. They were responsible for conducting the various rituals. Among these were twenty **Fetiales**, who were involved in the formal and intangible relations of the Roman people and their deities with foreign peoples and their Gods. Then there were the twenty **Sodales Titii** and twelve **Fratres Arvales** who were assigned to the cult of Dia, Goddess of the bright sky linked to the agricultural cycle. Then we had the twenty **Sodales Augustales**, priests of the cults of the different deified emperors. Finally, there were the two companies of twelve **Salii** who carried out the ritual processions linked to the war season and the two Confraternities of **Luperci** who celebrated the sacred race around the limits of the Palatine on the festival of Lupercalia.

Flamines, distinguished by their pointed apices, as part of a procession on the Augustan Altar of Peace

Own work, CC BY-SA 3.0 <https://creativecommons.org/licenses/by-sa/3.0>, via Wikimedia Commons, uploaded by Wolfgang Rieger.

The colleges documented their activities on the walls of the buildings in which they were located or on other supporting materials, mostly stone. These etchings kept their knowledge alive for hundreds of years, and it made it possible for us to know intimately about the life of those institutions of the ancient Roman state. The etchings included a list of donations received, lists of magistrates, reports of meetings, and much more.[43] Take for example, the College of the Fratres Arvales, which traced its foundation back to the Romulean age. Substantial documentation of this college's work for a period that goes from 732 to 994 ab U.C. is available to us even today. The college was made up of twelve lifetime members who were renewed by cooptation from the priests of Dia. Reports of their ceremonies were written on various objects and, more importantly, on the walls of the temple of the Goddess Dia outside the city, which was near the current city of Magliana, on the road to Fiumicino. Particularly exceptional is a marble fragment containing on both sides the report of the ceremonies held on the 27 and 28 May 218 C.E. (971 ab U.C.), which includes the sacrifices and the Carmi done. It is an incredibly important document for us because it provides information on the ancient rituals with sufficient details to recreate those ceremonies along with their associated rituals today. [44]

Functions of the Pontifical College

The Romans observed the *Ius Sacrum* (sacred law), which was based on ancient traditions and laws concerning the relationship between men and Gods, or rather between Rome and the Gods. They did this so that the ***Pax Deorum*** (the peace of the Gods) could be realized here on earth. Peace in this context meant a balanced condition incorporating all aspects, from the socio-economic to the political and religious. Although the Roman patricians were generally initiates, not everyone was able to understand the laws of the universe. Therefore, it was wisely decided to establish the sacred law so that Rome's renewal of the covenants with the deities would not be jeopardized. As sacred law, it would become part of the shared tradition, and thus it would be transmitted down to future generations as symbolical knowledge. ***Pietas*** thus ensured the welfare of the people as envisioned by the original patricians. Political and religious life were inseparable, and one could not live without the other. Therefore, in the cursus honorum, political and religious charges came to meet. The best-known case is that of the dictatorial judiciary, conferred in cases of crisis from the Senate to a prominent person. This magistrate held absolute power for six months, on the army, on the political bodies and religious institutions. The dictator was also known by the title of ***Magister Populi***. The intervention of Quintus Fabius Maximus in the religious affairs during the war against Hannibal is well known. The dictator carried out an ***advocatio*** on the Venus of Erice, and reestablished the ***Pax Deorum*** in the Roman system with the erection of a shrine in honor of Mens. Before him, there was the Consul Caius Flaminius, who lost the battle of the Trasimeno in an attempt to surprise the Punics with a daring action. As soon as Quintus Fabius Maximus assumed his office, he summoned the senators and explained to them that Flaminius had sinned more for recklessness rather than for impiousness. Flaminius attacked the Carthaginians without first taking the auspices and without first carrying out the necessary rites. Fabius then made sure that the Sibylline Books were consulted by the Decemvirs, dictated that Rome renew the vow to the God Mars because the Martial rites had remained unfinished, to dedicate the great games to Iuppiter and to erect a temple to Venus and Mens. Had Flaminius secured permissions via the appropriate rites, he would have secured victory over Hannibal. After the intervention of the expert Cunctator Fabius, the **venia** of the Goddess Venus was favorably manifested in Rome, which grew in its imperial power.[45]

The pontifical college was therefore made up of patricians who were experts in tradition. Some of these charges lasted an entire life, while others like that of the vestals had a maximum age limit, beyond which the priest or priestess was exonerated from their responsibilities to the state, which until then had provided them with a fixed salary. Other offices, such as that of the **Pontifex Maximus**, were conferred by the confraternities such as the **Auguri**, the **Flamines**, and the Vestals of the pontifical college, and these were chosen by the people. The task of a Pontifex is to create bridges with the astral world and to keep in direct communication with the Gods. The **Auguri** kept this contact through the interpretation of the flight of birds, the Haruspices from reading the bowels of the sacrificial victims, and the **Pontifex Maximus** by other secret means.

Among other things, the Pontifices had to be experts in astronomy because they produced the calendars and announced the holidays of the month. In the imperial times, this duty became a mere formality, since with the Cesarian reform of the calendar, all public festivals now followed the solar cycle, and every four years, the intercalation took place. All that was needed to be known in any year was whether it was an intercalation year or not. In the Republican era, the difficulties were greater since the calendar was lunar and therefore required more complex tracking. The cycle of the moon and the sun do not synchronize with each other,[46] and the Pontifex had the responsibility to reconcile the lunar and solar months. The lunar month is the time that the moon takes to orbit around the earth while the solar month is the time that the apparent motion of the sun due to earth's revolution, takes to cross one of the twelve imaginary portions of the sky, which we call signs and which were known by the ancients as the zodiac. The lunar month as we know, lasts about twenty-nine and a half days, while the solar month is about thirty days. The ancient Sumerians already felt the need to make the solar cycle coincide with the lunar one. Therefore, they created a lunisolar calendar in 4000 B.C.E., three thousand years before the foundation of Rome. The solar calendar year is 11 days longer than the sum of all days in the twelve lunar months and about 18 days shorter than thirteen lunations. So, the lunar months travel backward through the seasons in a cycle of 33 years, at the end of which the two cycles return to coincide, as it happens even today in the various lunar chronologies that are still in use around the world. The method used in the traditional calendar of the fathers consisted of the intercalation of entire lunar months, adopted for the season. The same system was also used in Mesopotamia. A decree of Hammurabi, dating back to 1700 B.C.E., says, "This year has a month interleaved. The coming month must be called according to Ululu."[47] In the same way in Rome, a September bis or an October bis could be presented, and so on. From the length of the day (i.e., from the duration of the sunlight in the sky), the Pontifex realized what season they were in. For example, if the day was not long enough, the month of Martius was not declared, but the Februarius was repeated as "Februarius bis." In fact, if March was declared in the lunar month preceding the entrance of the sun in Aries, and therefore before the spring equinox, it was not then possible to offer to God Mars the first fruits that belonged to him.

The Babylonians were also the first to adopt the eight-year cycle consisting of five common twelve-month years and three special years, which had thirteen months due to the additional interleaved month. It was then replaced by a nineteen-year cycle, in which the third, sixth, eighth, eleventh, fourteenth, seventeenth, and nineteenth were interleaved. The difference in the solar and lunar cycles was thus reduced to a minimum value of 0.00463 of a day. Also, in 432 B.C.E., Meton of Athens studied a cycle of nineteen years, consisting of twelve common years and seven interleaves. In Rome, the Republican age calendar included 355 days. Therefore, every two years, the month of February was interleaved, with a month of 22-23 days. This intercalation, however, created a discrepancy with both the lunar and solar cycles. So much so that Cicero, in describing how the Greeks were concerned to make the calendar coincide with the sun, criticizes the Roman calendar, which did not synchronize either with the sun or with the moon.[48] Caesar, in the creation of a new calendar, took a cue from the Egyptian calendar to make the months coincide again with the seasons, and even today apart from minor variations, the Gregorian calendar perfectly follows the previous one.

Being experts of the sacred law, the Pontifices had the task, as previously mentioned, of ensuring that the **Pax Deorum** flourished among men. Each divinity had specific times during the year when rituals for them had to be performed. The Pontifices systematically followed this ritual calendar and conducted the appropriate rituals on time. There were priesthoods and families that made daily offerings to specific divinities so that these Gods were constantly satisfied and they were perpetually favorable to the eternal city. Furthermore, a direct dialogue with the Gods was established through the augural and haruspical readings and through the Sibylline books, which were consulted by decemvirs on the orders of the Senate if important decisions were taken to tackle crises that would have questioned the future of Rome. In fact, the geese of the **Collis Capitolinus** and the whole Nature with its continuous messages were a means of continuous dialogue with the Gods. At the time of Numa, the Pontifices[49] were five. Then their number was raised to sixteen, both for a real need for more experts of sacred law and for "cabalistic" or, in other words, magical reasons, linked to this number sixteen. The college was also responsible for the preparation of the **Libri Sacerdotum Populi Romani Quiritium**, which were the maxims of rituals and ceremonies that were to be carried out according to sacred law to maintain the aforementioned **Pax Deorum**. The pontifical decrees and the responses obtained with the most varied practices were gathered in the **Commentarii Pontificum**, while the list of state magistrates and events of particular interest were respectively marked in the **Fasti** and in the **Annales Pontificum** or **Annales Maximi**.[50]

The Vestals were the most important female sacerdotal order in ancient Rome. A Roman wedding, in memory of the mythical event of the Abduction of the Sabine Women, was celebrated after a formal Captio, that is, after a fake kidnapping of the future wife, by the closest relatives of the husband, who were usually his brothers. Similarly, the Vestals entered the college with a ritual Captio carried out by the Pontifex. Despite the requirement of absolute chastity during the period of stay in the college from the age of eight to thirty-five, the Vestals were formal brides of the **Pontifex Maximus**, as we have previously explained.[51] Vigilantes of the sacred fire of Vesta, they enjoyed high respect and special rights, but if they violated their duties or their vows, they were punished with death. Their blood was sacred and therefore could not be shed. An executioner could not commit the unholy sacrilege of touching them to strangle them. So, they were buried alive if they violated absolute chastity and were heavily flogged if, by their fault, the sacred fire was extinguished. The temple of Vesta was the hearth of the city, and to ensure Rome's prosperity, its flames could never be extinguished. The cult of the Goddess Vesta seems to be of Indo-European origin. In fact, its Greek counterpart, Hestìa, has the same functions and keeps the name almost unaltered. When the Vestals were out and about the city, they were always escorted by a lictor, and at that time, if they met a condemned man who appealed to them for a pardon, they could pardon him. They also had the honor of sitting in the front row at the Colosseum and in the theaters. The cult of Vesta was very ancient. In fact, it was in practice amongst the inhabitants of the Roman region prior to the foundation of the city. As mentioned before, it was a Vestal, Rhea Silvia, who was coveted by the God Mars, to be the mother of the twins Romulus and Remus who founded Rome.

Flamines were the priests who dealt with individual cults. These priests were divided into major **Flamines** (Dialis, Martialis, and Quirinalis) and minor **Flamines** (Carmentalis, Cerialis, Falacer, Floralis, Furrinalis, Palatualis, Pomonalis, Portunalis, Volturnalis, Volcanalis).[52] They were responsible for ensuring that the ceremonies dedicated to the deities to which they were responsible were carried out. The Flamen Dialis took care of the cult and the rituals dedicated to Jupiter, the Dieus, or Deus Pater. Similarly, other **Flamines** took care of Mars and Quirinus. So, the major **Flamines** were concerned with the cult of the Gods of the Capitoline triad, while the other **Flamines**, who were called minor for purely conventional distinction and not in importance, dealt with other deities related to various specific aspects of daily life and the initiation. The **Flamines** were required to be married householders. In fact, each of the Flamen must have a partner and then be married to a Flaminica and must comply with precise rules of married life.

Clavus Annalis

An indispensable part of **Pietas** Romana was the **Clavus Annalis** ritual, which was one of the most important rites serving the peace between men and the Gods. This rite consisted of establishing a will. According to the unwritten ancient law, "Lex Vetusta," every year the chief magistrate had to implant a nail in the cell walls of the temple of Jupiter Capitolinus. According to historian Cincius (Titus Livius 7.3.7), the ceremony of sticking the nail would have had an Etruscan origin and would serve the count of the years.[53] Marta Sordi (1925 - 2009), an Italian historian and academic claimed that the clavifixio[54] serves to indicate the pledge of divine assistance assured in Rome, so it was a ritual required to establish **Pax Deorum**.[52] In the imperial age, during the Ides of September, the protection and the aeternitas for Rome was invoked by the consul and by Augustus. Three hundred ninety-six years after the foundation of Rome, an extraordinary clavifixio, called **pacis deum exposcendae causa** took place (Titus Livius 7.22). This undermines the theories of historians such as Alföldi and Cincius, who gave to it just a chronological value and at the same time confirms the theory of the historian Sordi that this rite really had a magic-apotropaic function.[53] The purpose of this ritual was to identify and remove the negative influences from the past, the proof of which was the aforementioned special clavifixio carried out by Augustus to put an end to an epidemic in the city. As to the time during the year when this rite must have been performed, some considerations need to be made. The consuls of the first republic took office in September, probably during the **Idus**,[54] and celebrating the pax with Jupiter was to assert the power that they were granted.[55] Some scholars have noted a need to equalize the levels of sovereignty, hence the necessity of the dictator in times of crisis, since there were only the **Intercessio Tribunicia** and the **Provocatio Ad Populum** as resolving elements of imbalance (lack of **Pax Deorum**) powers that however invested the middle and lower social strata. The case of the **Praetor Maximus** that after some social unrest obtained with the ritual of the clavifixio the realignment of the misguided minds is emblematic and shows that situations to be expiated can manifest themselves in political-social tensions.[56] By fixing the nail in the stone block of the temple cell, the desire to keep the ***Pax Deorum*** stable was established. A pleasant gesture, but not just a gesture but a statement of the will of the power of the highest magistracy to maintain the order of Rome. So, this important ritual had both the magical element and the socio-political aspect to it.

Capitulum IV
De Initiationis Mysteriisque

Philosopher's Path

The human spirit inherently yearns for the Truth. To realize it, some depend on the purest rationalism of an atheist and others on the unbridled mysticism of a religious fanatic. Wise men, though adhere to the wisdom of the ancient Romans, *in medio stat virtus*, virtue lies in the middle. Therefore, they choose a healthy balance between the two extremes. In the ancient world, these seekers were called philosophers. They start on their inner journey using the power of human reason, but they eventually transcend into something higher. Often, these individuals were associated with temples, but the more enlightened ones managed to overcome the limitations of rationality and be initiated into the mysteries. The philosophers detach themselves from the profane crowd before the temple, pouncing up the stairs thanks to the use of **Ratio**, reason. Then they learn to abandon the **Ratio** in favor of the **Mens**, an inner divine apparatus that allows them to come in contact with their own Genius, **Daimon**. **Mens** is the contraction of *meus ens*, my inner being, which is the **Numen** of the person. **Ratio** and **Mens** help the Philosophers ascend to the Truth, which starts in the temple, takes them through the mysteries, and finally brings them back into the temple.

Therefore, the mysteries are an important aspect of the Roman tradition. Pythagoras, the Greek philosopher, was initiated in the Egyptian temples. Another and probably better known Greek philosopher was Socrates, whose speeches and forma mentis are typical of the Pythagorean thought, so much so that some late-antique authors call him Pythagorean. Biographer, essayist, and philosopher Plutarch was initiated into the Dionysian mysteries, and in his last years, he became a priest at the temple of Delphi. Cicero, the statesman, orator, prose stylist, lawyer, and philosopher, was into augural mysteries. Apuleius, the prose writer, rhetorician, and philosopher, was into the mysteries of both Isis and Osiris. Philosopher Celsus, author of the famous critical work "The True Word" was initiated into mysteries as well. Even during the era of the Byzantine Empire, there was the philosopher and mathematician Hypatia of Alexandria who was not only initiated into the mysteries of Isis but also into certain therapeutic ones.

Shakko, Relief found in Neumagen near Trier, a teacher with three discipuli. Around 180–185 CE. Photo of casting in Pushkin museum, Moscow.

Shakko, CC BY-SA 3.0 <https://creativecommons.org/licenses/by-sa/3.0>, via Wikimedia Commons.

Initiation into a mystery path under the guidance of an achieved teacher was and even today is the only path for one to complete one's philosophical education within the Roman Tradition. To better understand the concepts related to initiation, it is first necessary to understand how the phases of a man's spiritual life were organized within Roman society. During ancient times, the path to initiation depended on one's social standing obtained by birth. One could be born a slave, a free man, or a citizen.

A slave could be born as such, become one for unpaid debts, or forced into slavery because he was a prisoner of war. Any slave had to redeem his freedom by serving a family of wealthy citizens. The servitude still allowed one to save money and buy his way out by purchasing another slave to replace him. While he was with the family of his masters, he also learned the Latin language if he did not know it already. The slaves who became free were called freedmen and integrated immediately and perfectly into society. They were better than many children of free and wealthy citizens accustomed to having everything and sometimes inept in procuring goods and wealth. Known are the names of many freedmen who became skilled traders after completing their servitude. Some were enriched to the point they became knights of the Roman Res Publica. The emancipation of a slave was a real initiation into Roman society and an opportunity to eventually become **Cives Romanus**.

Then there were generic free men. They were non-citizens who usually lived at the borders of the Roman empire and were considered naïve or, in Roman terms, without Genius, **Daimon**[57]. Most of these people had foreign origins and therefore practiced cults, which were different from those that the Romans adhered to.

The **Cives Romanus** or Roman citizens constituted the majority of the Roman population. They were the chief followers of the Roman tradition. At the age of seventeen, the young Romans abandoned the childish **toga** to assume the virile one. They became **viri** instead of **homines**. **Vir** is the one who embodies the *vis*, that is the strength, *homo* is he who is made of *humus*, of mud. From the *vis* of the *vir* or virgo comes the word *virtus*. With the assumption of citizenship, a man obtained political and religious rights. Included among the religious ones was the freedom to practice in private the Roman traditional path for their spiritual development, and therefore the man became a priest of himself. If he lived in the family of his birth, he was still subject to paternal authority, which too encompassed the religious sphere. If he went to live alone or set up another family, he became his *iure Pater Familias*. The *Cives* was a gentile, a man who knew the qualities of his Genius, **Daimon**. Nowadays, those who call themselves pagan rather than gentile must still free themselves from a stereotyped nomenclature born with a pejorative purpose in late antiquity. It is to be recognized that today's pagan has freed himself from the schematic slavery of the contemporary social mosaic. He wants to emphasize rustic and natural purity. Therefore, he is a man who strives for freedom, but he still belongs to the category of the naive because he does not know the qualitative condition of his own **Numen**. The knowledge of one's *numen* is known only when one acquires a particular awareness related to a specific stage of inner purification.

Initiation

The initiation is a philosophical rebirth for the aspiring apprentice. It is the beginning of a new inner phase that replaces outdated intellectual and spiritual conditions. The ancient priestly wisdom of the Roman tradition is a product of thousands of years of experience. This knowledge is not written anywhere but is handed down from the teacher priest to his apprentice through experiential learning. This traditional teaching methodology takes the apprentice through seven fundamental stages that are revealed to him during his education. All those who enter the path of learning will have particular experiences, which are clear indications to the teacher that the student was able to overcome certain barriers and therefore ready to move on to the next stage. The Pontifices and the initiator teachers know well these experiences because they have themselves experienced them in the past, and therefore they can recognize the achieved development of a neophyte. These indications obviate the need to get the teacher's sycophantic attention and instead require that the apprentice focus on practical action as guided by his teacher to build the relationship with his **Numen** and have concrete experiences that advance him to higher stages. There are many different types of initiation. There is the initiation for the novice, who is just starting up the spiritual path after taking on the virile **toga**. Then there is the priestly initiation, which takes the advanced student into the temple. In every initiation, the initiatory path is divided into two main phases. The first is the lunar phase, and the second is the solar phase. Apuleius was first initiated into the mysteries of Isis and later to the Osirean mysteries. So, in the Roman calendar, the sacred festivals of Juno are celebrated at the new moon and first quarter moon, and then those of Jupiter are held at the full moon.

Neophytes start their journey with lunar initiation, during which they symbolically become the moons of their teacher, who enlightens them with his wisdom. The students who are focused, sincere, and receptive to their teacher's guidance gradually absorb the sunlight of teacher's wisdom to illuminate the mental darkness surrounding them and wax from a new moon beginner to a full moon advanced student and thus complete their lunar initiation. For some, it takes few years of work and, for others, a lifetime. In either case, that knowledge remains impressed in his soul, and the student will find himself spiritually advanced compared to the profane masses. One must understand the outer physical framework to be able to experience the sublimated inner essence. The moon phase of initiation imposes this requisite outer structure. If the student skips or disowns this step in the urge to quickly get to higher levels, she will disturb her mental balance and become mad. There are certain additional characteristics that a student must possess. Listening is very important for those who want to learn. Pythagoras obliged his disciples to years of silence before starting them on the Apollonian mathematics. She never profanes the teachings received but reflects her teacher's love for society and so is a source of help for the uninitiated ordinary people, giving them wise and thoughtful advice as necessary. She accepts constructive criticism. She works hard and does not let sloth inhibit her spiritual progress. One has to have tremendous willpower to stay the course on this path, and one will not have that willpower unless one has overcome the desire for inanition inherent in the seed of obscure animal pleasures nourished by the ghosts of concupiscence. Finally, and probably most importantly, the temple's doors are opened only to those on the side of justice and goodness. The ancient initiations were not for the poor in spirit, but they rewarded those beggars of fiery wisdom who had all these necessary characteristics.

The solar initiation succeeds the lunar one. Here the disciple concretizes hes detachment to passions and begins the path to her spiritual realization. The virtues of **Pietas** are incarnated to reach the condition of the shining sun. The knowledge acquired in the previous phase makes it possible to be reborn like the winter sun. She is surely a sun, but still too weak and small to bring a renewed spring. She must grow to rise more and more in the heavens until she achieves the heroic state of the summer sun. Thus, she becomes a Magister, an individual who can create the intellectual light from the magnetic energy she develops. Like Hercules, Ulysses, Perseus, and the other countless heroes of the Greek-Roman mythology, she will have to do great works to achieve the squaring of the circle, a balanced state within her inner self. The word of the solar initiate is more conscientious since she knows the importance of the **verbum**. She becomes increasingly measured in her speech because when the sun is reborn, it is Angerona's feast, the

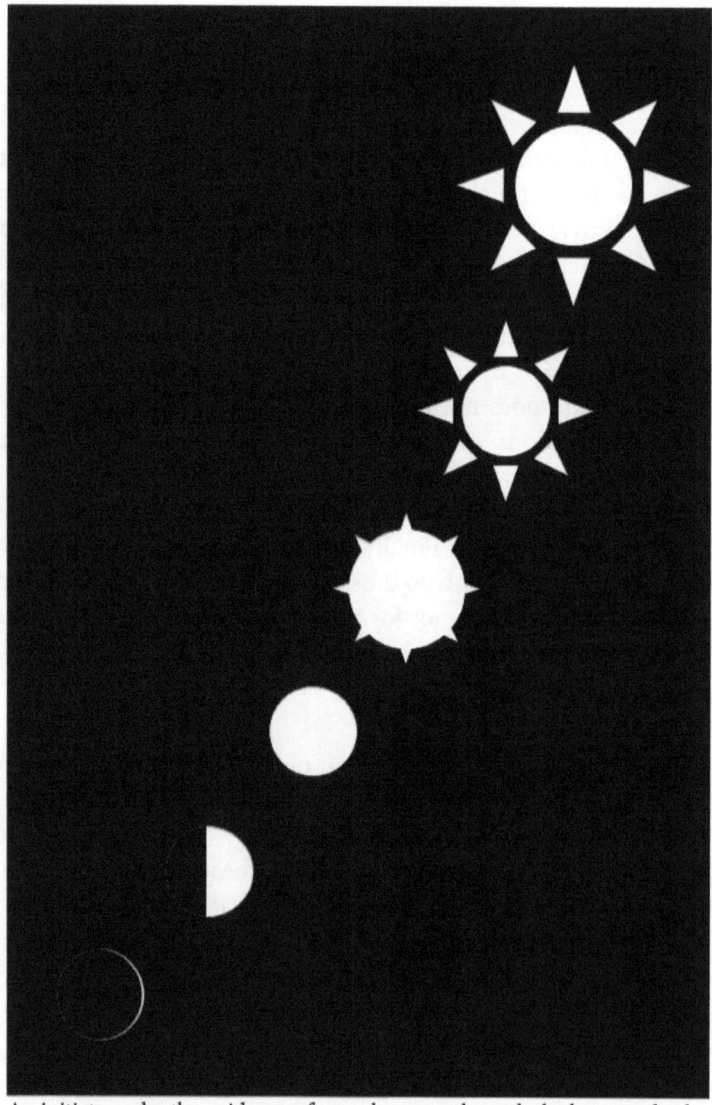
An initiate under the guidance of a teacher goes through the lunar and solar phases of education.

Domina Silentii. In the Pythagorean Magna Graecia, mathematicians had delved into the Apollonian mysteries. The Roman Pontifices in the imperial age assumed as a tutelary deity a Solar ***Numen***, so Augustus chose Apollo, Nero the Sun, Decio preferred Mithra, and Aurelianus renewed the cult of the Sol Invictus. Very few ancient initiates speak of how the solar path is developed. Apuleius stresses the impossibility of expressing the wonder of the Osirean mysteries, the Pythagoreans pass on the rules of the Acousmatics, but they avoid mentioning those of the mathematicians, and so on. They understand that truth is an intelligence that protects itself by revealing itself only to the deserving silent. Therefore, Macrobius points out that explaining the myths and their mysteries to everyone is akin to putting the Goddesses of wisdom on the street, obliging them to prostitute themselves. For the sake of sacred meritocracy, the initiates of the mysteries do not profane their knowledge. We have to add an important observation here. While the truth is an intelligence that never reveals itself to the chatterers so as to ensure that it does not become profane, many people, by happenstance, grasp small morsels of it. They misuse what little they know to feel important. They act in the name of their own pride, which always results in a punishment that manifests as an incorrect view of things in their minds. These petty desecrators are swindlers who hunt for naive who unfortunately become their subjects. These false teachers become impediments in the paths of their followers, who never attain their solar initiation. Blameworthy are the profaners of the temple's internal practices, who act with the intent of damaging the priestly wisdom.

True wisdom practices are only transmitted in person, and no one who knows explains them to anyone else. In fact, the mystery wisdom process does not happen by teaching but by recognition. The teacher gives his student certain rituals to perform. The disciple puts into practice these rituals, and by doing so, he obtains the mystery wisdom when he is ready for it. During this process, when he talks to his guide and presents his understanding of how to realize the mystery for his teacher's review, his teacher simply confirms or negates his understanding. At best, the teacher gives the student some pearls of wisdom so that if there is cleanliness and rectitude in the student, he will receive from his own ***Numen*** the right path for the conquest of the desired prize. From this, we can deduce that there cannot be a written practice that conveys a mystery, and that every profaned practice is a false deviant from the ***Veritas***. The teacher's task is to love, give the means, evaluate and recognize the student's progress. Unfortunately, nowadays, sloth and indolence reign over reason, which is why the sapient system of the ancient temple finds it difficult to manifest itself to today's vulgar society. Ours is indeed a sick age, where everything is due, and nothing is to be conquered, and where the teacher is doubted and criticized because he neglects to fulfill the burdens of his pupils. This is the time of pigs who stuff themselves with pearls only to satisfy the instinctive pleasure of swallowing, yet this is also the moment for the heroes.

But who is a hero today? He is the one who works hard to embody the ***Pietas***, the body of virtuous values, which he willfully undertakes to transform himself from ***homo*** to ***vir***. He takes on this arduous journey not for personal glory but for the restoration of a correct meritocratic spiritual system, from which will emerge a renewed social order, which will replace the impulsive behavior of our age with a healthy commitment to society.

It must be kept in mind that initiation consists, fundamentally, in the fulfillment of a gesture to move from a previous individual condition to a new awareness. Therefore, initiations include not just those in the temple, but also that of domestic ritual practices. These include the assumption of the virile ***toga*** as the initiation into religious life, the first sexual intercourse as the initiation into the erotic life, marriage as the initiation into the life of a householder, and so on. Every divinity corresponds to a force identified in nature and may have associated initiations. Different initiations may exist for different cults. These various initiations are useful to become aware of how their associated divinities operate in nature.

Thus, in ancient Rome, there were several initiatory colleges, from the Augural to the Arval, where the entrants became experts in managing specific forces. So, matrons, for example, in addition to entering into a new life with the contraction of marriage, were initiated in the mysteries of Bona Dia to learn how to manage the sacred energies that develop in the family and to best perform their own function peacefully. Similarly, the legionnaire was initiated into the martial cult of the legion, which developed around the sacred insignia and so on. All these other initiations, which took place in the appropriate temples, were specializations related to the Genial qualities of the individual, and they did not interfere with the initiatory path started with the transition to the gentile condition but enriched it.

Practicing Roman Religion Today

Is it possible to practice the Roman tradition nowadays? Certainly, there are various associations, in Italy and abroad, that deal with Roman tradition. It is up to the individual to explore and evaluate until she finds the right conditions and suitable companions. Surely honest and pious women will be approached by those like them while rogues, crooks, defamers, and improvised traditionalists will attract and keep with them either those with similar tendencies or the naive ones who unfortunately fall for their shams. The Aristotelian principle, **similia similibus**, which means "everyone is attracted and attracts people similar to himself", is very true indeed. Those who have evolved within themselves will approach evolved people, and the involute will find in their search, involute people and will be associated with them, sometimes despising groups only because they are envious. Gold associates with gold. Silver aspires to gold because it is next to silver in the scale of values but better. Lead groups with lead, and sometimes it despises gold because it is unattainable from its current condition. When one enters a human group, attends its congregations, perceives a sincere harmony with its members, to all intents and purposes, one experiences, however mild, an initiatory experience and begins to think with a new form of mind. We approach the sacred based on the lessons we receive, but how can we know if those notions are correct or not?

Unfortunately, it is easy to meet swaggerers who are improvised priests of great experience, so you must proceed with caution. The first thing to analyze is whether the group is cohesive or not. Then look at the real mental wholesomeness of its members. If they are a group of heterogeneous madmen, who are so unbalanced even in their approach to dialogue, that they cannot even respect the current language form, well then, beware of those and get ready for a noble escape, in the manner of the **Rex Sacrorum** on the 24th February. On the other hand, when you meet people whose cleanliness is perceived from afar, whose aura reassures you and whose wisdom seems to be acquired by experience rather than by reading, then approach them hieratically like you do at the altars and behave piously as if you were talking to an occult God. At the same time, verify if these people behave with righteousness and justice amongst themselves, that they are people who avoid gossip and traducing about other groups or people, and last but not least if they are upright with you, then cultivate a sincere friendship and begin to distinguish precious metals from ignoble ones. You must watch your behavior as well. Avoid wickedness and ignominy. Do not take advantage of the righteous people, for they are precious, and they will punish you by concealing their light and never give you the slightest consideration.

Although we have explained that the disciple is moon of the Teacher, it is good to clarify some things. No matter what type of grouping one decides to join, one should not be forced to be receptive to that group's spiritual guidance. One must be free to approach it albeit, piously, that is, with good intentions. When one thinks she has found the sun suitable for her and if she considers the chosen preceptor's teachings to be valid, then she can follow his teachings and undertake the path of discipleship. The whole process is no different than how one chooses to specialize in a specific field at a university for the desired career path.

A student at university who carefully listens to the teacher gets the best grades, so will a student at the temple get the best results during her spiritual path, without needing nepotism or such favors because, in the end, it's the Gods who judge and the initiates respect the divine will. Some people, approaching Traditional Roman Religion, arrogate the right to question its traditional rules that for millennia have been practiced in the priestly casts of ethnic religions worldwide. They invent even older religions, elaborating daring and flawlessly spoiled interpretations, only to give space to their pride. Those individuals who feel wiser than all the ancient priests of every age commit the sin of pride by jumping to teach others without ever having learned the basics of spiritual knowledge themselves. You cannot pretend to teach the history of religions in the faculty of letters without obtaining an undergraduate degree. A subject can only be taught after having learned and applied it in one's life. New insights and new knowledge can always be reached, but first, it is always necessary to learn the basics of science and its history. Otherwise, there will never be progress.

When one decides to access the practices of a community, it is necessary at first to succeed in becoming a part of it; just like in ancient Rome, citizenship was a right that was gained. It is important to try to follow the teachings of the chosen center. Sometimes, after a while, you may realize that you made a wrong choice or prefer a different community, similar to some university students who change their major or guide midway through their degree. This is a legitimate thing to do, but the important thing is to always know how to cultivate virtue within oneself, and even when you change your path, you must do it in style and not like a yokel; otherwise, the derogatory meaning of the word pagan[58] takes shape at the expense of the value of resistance, coherence, and virtue of the inhabitant of the **Pagus**.

Many people build **Lararia**,[59] where they live their deepest spirituality, but they constantly desecrate them by sending their images around the net or showing them to every visitor of their home, as if they were to initiate them into arcane mysteries. In all of this, there is only a sense of pride that seeks the approval of others. As for the actual practice, they download prayers from the net, exhume them from old texts and do such other similar things. These sorts of things are practice without preparation. We are confused when we see the wishes fulfilled, but they soon vanish. This is because the rituals have been performed incorrectly. However, we make the error of concluding that the misfortunes that follow are due to evil forces that are hurled at us because of practicing these rituals. We make this false assumption without understanding that the negative results stem from practicing the rituals without preparation. Chastity, fasting, and prayer are the three fundamental rules for practicing traditional rituals. Be it half a day or an entire day, but it must be done. You do not perform a ritual with a full stomach. For the prayer, you do not use random orations. It is always good to have a healthy reference that gives sound advice. Most importantly, those who want to follow a spiritual path must do it for the spirit, not to obtain material goods. It is good to pray for the well-being of the people we love, for health, for the intellectual light. In life, we face many difficulties and are afflicted; we are brought to approach the Gods. It is wise to ask the Gods to be cleansed of wickedness. It is good to pray for our own **Numen** so that it may give us the strength to do

Claus Ableiter, Lararium (Sacrificial altar and niche for figurines of Gods), found in Pompeii, 79 AD.

Claus Ableiter, CC BY-SA 3.0 <https://creativecommons.org/licenses/by-sa/3.0>, via Wikimedia Commons.

the deeds of our life with virtue and not to pray for him to solve for us. The gentile uses the **vis** to be the **vir**, the man or **virgo**, the woman. The Roman man takes control of his life; he is the proponent of his destiny, not the stars. This inner strength comes from the sacred inner fire of the spirit, which gives the energy and light necessary for a satisfying life.

We suggest the rite to one's own Genius for those who really want to approach the traditional practice. Pray to your own **Numen** chastely and purely. It is not necessary to pray mystically every day at all times. It is more useful to pray well and rarely than often and badly. Refrain from venereal pleasures and meats before practicing. We do not perform rituals without being sure about their purpose and performance details. In fact, they are only conquered in the temple. We suggest the Orphic hymn to one's Genius to get from him help, good advice, and the strength to face difficult times.

Lararium of a Modern-Day Pietas Adherent

LXXII. TO THE DÆMON, OR GENIUS[60]

The Fumigation from Frankincense.

Thee, mighty-ruling, Dæmon dread, I call, mild Jove [Zeus], life-giving, and the source of all:

Great Jove, much-wand'ring, terrible and strong, to whom revenge and tortures dire belong.

Mankind from thee, in plenteous wealth abound, when in their dwellings joyful thou art found;

Or pass thro' life afflicted and distress'd, the needful means of bliss by thee supprest.

Tis thine alone endu'd with boundless might, to keep the keys of sorrow and delight.

O holy, blessed father, hear my pray'r, disperse the seeds of life-consuming care; With fav'ring mind the sacred rites attend, and grant my days a glorious, blessed end.

Whoever wants to evolve and find his right path will have to purify himself. The ancient Romans scrupulously observed the three main phases of the moon, namely **Kalendae** or the New Moon, **Nonae** or the First Quarter Moon, and **Idus** the Full Moon. On these three days every lunar month, abundant body lavages are performed. There is ablution in the morning, and in the evening. During the day the foods from dead animals are avoided, and the vital ones such as fruits and vegetables are preferred. In the morning, incense is offered, and flowers are placed on the altar of the **Lararium** as long as you keep yourself chaste before approaching it. Those who wish may recite prayers to Juno at **Kalendae** and at the **Nonae**, while Jupiter will be prayed to at the **Idus**. Honor the Gods and avoid getting corrupted by desire and asking for things. In fact, desire destroys the Will, which is the flight of the body. Solstices and Equinoxes are held in honor of the Sun. Here too, avoid eating dead animals during the day, keep chaste and pray to the Solar **numen** to purify yourself from your evils and show yourself the way of Salus.

Unknown, Photograph of a first-century Roman Lararium from the House of the Vettii in Pompeii. The astral serpent at the bottom represents Genius Loci.

Unknown, CC BY-SA 2.5 <https://creativecommons.org/licenses/by-sa/2.5/deed.en>, via Wikimedia Commons.

If you know pious people, ethically healthy and full of wisdom, frequent them. Practice and above all study. If you want to meditate, do not lose yourself in unnecessary mental exercises, but follow the Pythagorean teachings expressed in the Golden Verses. Well-worked thinking is **Mens sana in corpose sano** and allows a better effect in cathartic rites. If you want to evolve spiritually, pray to Minerva during the Minervalia, the one who supports the heroes who commit themselves to the way back to the monade. From 18th to 25th March, be on a vegetarian diet, practice absolute chastity, and from 19th to 24th March, pray every morning the Goddess of Wisdom so that you are shown the way to evolve in the virtues of **Pietas**. The good and pure will have replies, and they will be well recognized by divine action. The malicious will be misled or, at best, be ignored. These pearls will certainly be useful to the pure, useless to the wicked.

To approach the traditional Roman way, we suggest studying the Greek and Latin classics. In particular, the Neoplatonists are preferred. A simple manual of the history of the Roman religion can be useful to know the basics of the ancient cult. To the sacred writings of Iliad, Odyssey, Aeneid, Eclogues, Georgics, Theogony, Homeric Hymns, and Orphic Hymns add the works of Emperor Flavius Claudius Julianus, who infamously was called the apostate.

Here is a list of some suggested additional ancient texts:

The Art of listening, Plutarch

Delphic dialogues, Plutarch

On the true doctrine, Celsus

The cave of the nymphs, Porfirio

On the Gods and the world, Sallust

Saturnalia, Macrobius

Somnium Scipionis, Cicero

Comment on the Somnium Scipionis, Macrobius

The golden ass, Apuleius.

Among the authors of modern times, we recommend studying the works of Giordano Bruno and the Neoplatonists. Remarkable is, for example, "The occult philosophy or the magic" of Agrippa for its continuous references to profound ancient theological knowledge. Of the many contemporary works that discusses the Roman world, we find the work of Enrico Montanari, such as "*Roma. Momenti di una presa di coscienza culturale,*" methodologically brilliant. The book is full of academic rationalism, which is sublimated with analysis of history. It is very useful in understanding the approach based on the mutually interacting physical and metaphysical variables that the Romans undertook during the Second Punic War.

The Mysteries

Mystery rituals are an important part not only of the Greco-Roman religion but also of many ethnic religions of the world. These were essentially the initiation of individuals into a path of elevation from the human worldly plane to the divine realm. These rites, ceremonies, and experiences were usually kept secret and divulged slowly to the individual as he or she progressed along the path of higher knowledge. Such cults include the tantra religion of the Hindus, mysteries of Isis and Osiris in Egypt, the Adoniac of Syrian cults, the Persian mysteries, and the Phrygian Cabeirian mysteries. Many mystery cults developed in ancient Rome, but there is something we can particularly call as the Roman mystery tradition, and we have more than enough historical evidence to resurrect the same. One is genetically predisposed to more easily absorb the traditions of one's ancestors compared to those of others. Within the academic circles of esotericism, this has been affirmed by more than a few scholars. That being said, there is a common ground where the essence of all these mystery cults meets. While a comparative study of various mystery traditions is an interesting subject, in this book we are focusing on one of the three primary mysteries of Roman tradition, namely those of Saturn. The other two primary mysteries are those of Venus and Fortuna. The Mystery of Saturn is about time, the second one is about **Amor**, the son of Venus, and the third one about Fortuna explores destiny. We also talk briefly about Hercules' Mystery, which is an important one for any initiate's development. But first, to participate in any traditional Roman practice, one must receive basic initiation. A detailed discussion of these mysteries is beyond the scope of this book. Actually, talking about them is beyond the scope of any book because they have to be experienced under the guidance of one's teacher.

The First Mystery

According to the opinion of many authoritative scholars, including the well-known Julius Evola, the Roman tradition does not provide for any initiation rites, but in reality, all Roman citizens were initiated when they reached seventeen years of age. This was restricted to only the patricians, but after the plebian movement, it was available to all **Cives Romanus**. These initiation ceremonies were performed at a certain time of the year. When the constellation of the Great Kite[61] arose, and on the fifth day before the entrance of the sun into Aries, that is around the Spring Equinox - 17th March time frame[55], the Liberalia ceremonies were celebrated. Rituals were performed in honor of God Liber, the one who frees from the chains of materiality and a childlike naivety. On this day, the boys assumed the virile *toga* and placed a *virgulto* in the **Lararium** in the presence of the **Penates**.[56] The *virgulto* is a statue representing the person who is assuming the *toga* in that ceremony. This initiation gave the Roman **Cives** the right to participate in the rituals prescribed by tradition. The ceremony is not an initiation into adulthood, which as per Roman law, was determined based on puberty. Post puberty, one was permitted to what was allowed for adults, like contracting marriage or dedicating oneself to work and war. The virile *toga* was different and indicated not the biological adulthood but that of virtue, since the *vir*, unlike *homo*, was the one who possessed the *virtus*. Their initiator was a martial priest, who, in addition to giving them basic instructions on relevant sacred things, would dress them in a *toga* marked with a red stripe: fire and God's color. It was called virile *toga* because it distinguished the initiates by the *homines* (common men made from mud, *humus*), while characterizing them for their strength, *vis* acquired by *Ignis*, the Fire. Each of them has become a *vir* who, with his actions and his ritual offerings of incense will come to embody the typical *virtus* of every true Roman. Romulus, son of Mars, initiated the first Romans under the auspices of Jupiter. Subsequently, in this manner, the young Romans followed a procession behind a large phallus, a martial and solar symbol being led up to the Capitol. Here, near the temple of Jupiter, they concluded their rite of initiation with the obtainment of the virile *toga* to the presence of the community. At the end of the day's festivities, a matron with the reputation of having honorable behavior and marital fidelity covered the big phallus with a cloth. The meaning of this ceremony for Romans is that the phallus was associated with the generating power of the male strength and they saw a need to put it under sacral control. There was nothing obscene in that ritual.

But how was such a valuable thing called *virtus* achieved? Were those seeking the *toga* have to overcome any barrier, or was it simply given to anyone who was a descendant of a Roman citizen? If we look at the ritual calendar, we can see that February, which is the prior month in which the civil initiation is conducted, is full of purification rituals related to Goddess Febris, who purifies the body from evils. February is also a propitious time for the initiates to be welcomed, a season in which the rebirth takes place as the sun takes its revenge over darkness when in the spring equinox, the dominion of sunlight begins to surpass the darkness of the night. From the *Nonae* of February, first lunar quarter phase to the *Idus* of March, full moon of the month the initiates go through a purification period, which could be referred to as a ritual preparation for the initiation of Liberalia. On 19th of March, the Minerval period begins, and on 21st March, the Sun enters Aries. The initiation on March 17th could also be followed by a rite of Aries that would begin under the sign of Minerva with the necessary preparation through the lustration of the weapons of the Salii and of the ritual objects used by the initiate who is a priest unto himself.[57] This period would end at the *Idus* of April or with the feasts of the Fordicidia, sacred to Tellus, also understood as the land or the body on which the initiate would operate in this period of time. Like in many ancient traditions, the Aries period, which falls in March, marks for the Romans the beginning of the sacred year and is an initiatory ritual period. Ulysses clung to an Aries to escape from the cave of Polyphemus, the cyclops who wanted to devour him and his companions and can symbolically be understood as one's animal instincts. In Egypt, the priests conducted the rite of Aries, as did their Chaldean predecessors. The Abrahamic faiths have inculcated this type of ritual as well. This is evident in the Jewish ritual of Lent and the Christian ritual of Easter.

The Mysteries of Hercules

Among the various mysteries of Rome, the one of Hercules has special importance in the education and development of an initiate because Hercules represents both the phases of the initiation process, namely first the Lunar phase, where the initiate "receives" and then the Solar phase during which the initiate becomes his own sun or Teacher after having overcome certain obstacles in his path.

The mystery of Hercules was among the first cults that were brought into Rome. The mystery revolves around his altar and the family that holds the mystery, the Potitii. Hercules is called Heracles by the Greeks. It is name the mythical hero got from the moment when he becomes the servant of Hera, who is the Goddess of the moon and represents the feminine aspect of the microcosm. Therefore Hercules is a servant of the soul and carries out his deeds to purify it, and he becomes a hero because he fights for divine love.[58] He begins his deeds as a child, strangling the two serpents that Juno sent to his cradle. The child Hercules is the symbolic representation of the initiate. Since the child does not speak, he cannot reveal the secret mysteries, and by being small and pure, he does not know malice and is chaste. In the same way, Mithra is born in a cave from a virgin, Horus in a reed bed from the virgin Isis in the presence of the God Thoth. Another great undertaking of Hercules is killing a Nemean lion that threatened the flocks that he was grazing. For having saved Thebes, the sovereign Creonus gave him his daughter Megara as a wife, but soon Hercules massacred their innocent sons. He had to undertake the twelve labors to atone for the guilt. These are nothing but symbols of the twelve deeds that man must perform in order to be accepted in the Olympus where the immortal Gods live.

In the Indo-European traditions, the concept of the divinization of man is an accepted belief. The path to divinity is intercepted by fate, which lashes out against anyone who attempts this. We know not of any hero who succeeded without surmounting arduous difficulties. Romulus had to kill his brother to

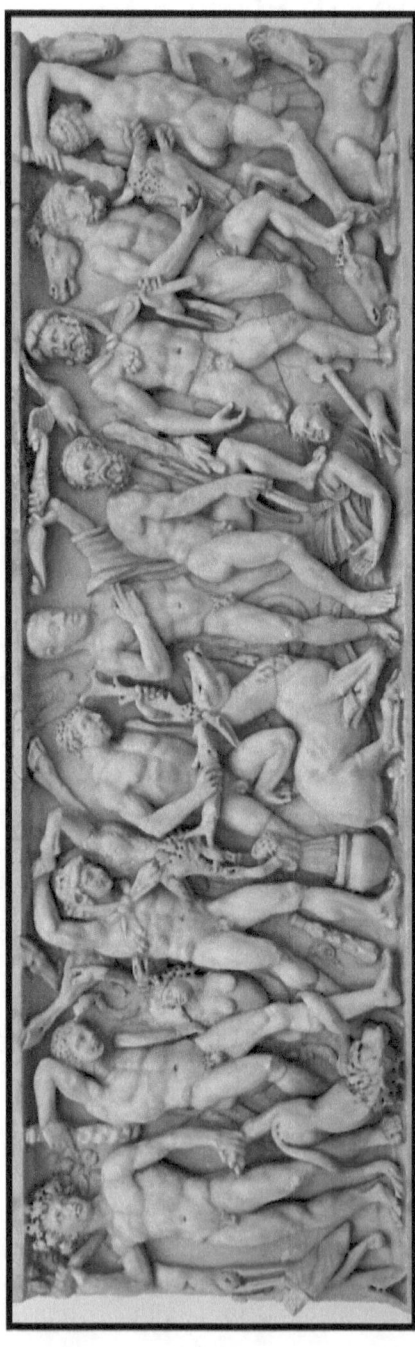

Marie-Lan Nguyen, Front panel from a sarcophagus with the Labours of Heracles: from left to right, the Nemean Lion, the Lernaean Hydra, the Erymanthian Boar, the Ceryneian Hind, the Stymphalian birds, the Girdle of Hippolyta, the Augean stables, the Cretan Bull and the Mares of Diomedes. Luni marble, Roman artwork from the middle 3rd century CE.

Marie-Lan Nguyen, Public domain, via Wikimedia Commons.

make a dream a reality. Aeneas had to face the wrath of the ruthless Goddess Juno. Ulysses had to face monsters of all kinds and the anger of Poseidon himself, and he found the way to salvation only because of the powerful Goddess Minerva, beloved daughter of Zeus, the father of all Gods and men.

Carole Raddato, Saturn with head protected by winter cloak, holding a scythe in his right hand, fresco from the House of the Dioscuri at Pompeii, Naples Archaeological Museum.

Carole Raddato, CC BY-SA 2.0 <https://creativecommons.org/licenses/by-sa/2.0>, via Wikimedia Commons.

The Mysteries of Saturn

There is an interesting work of the neo-Platonic pagan writer Macrobio called "Saturnalia," where the arcanum is discussed. The mysteries of Saturn precede the existence of time and space. These were kept for a long time in the region of Latium. Mythology tells us that Saturn came to Rome to teach the inhabitants of the region agriculture and its secrets. The God hid in the region of Latium or Latium a Latere according to Ovid, and his teachings are what constitute the real mystery. In fact, the alchemical phrase in latin says **Visita Interiora Terrae, Rectificando Invenies Occultum Lapidem**, reach into the material earth to find your essence. The development of the subtle bodies, namely soul, intelligence and spirit begins with this research. Time marks positive moments and negative moments and knowing how to recognize them is necessary for recognizing the right moment for doing anything. For these reasons, the Greeks called him Cronos. Time and space are contemporary and play an existential cycle. According to the most advanced scientific theories, the universe is born of the primordial atom, Chaos, and expands. From that moment, the matter is ordered, and a sort of cosmic breath or the wheel of Fortuna is established, which will eventually return to the Chaos of the primordial atom. Time and matter will collapse. All this is due to chance, the profane name of the Goddess Fortuna. Those who understand the rules of Fortuna are abstracted from the dimension of Saturn and transcend space and time.

By understanding the laws of agriculture, we come to the understanding of the laws that regulate the evolution of the individual. It is in the physical body that the seed of wisdom and knowledge is to be planted. The farmers in ancient times, and some even of the present day, follow the trend of the moons to know the timing of sowing, care, and harvest. The damp earth allows a better growth of the plant. The seed produced by the fruit must die to give life to the new plant. The first act that the farmer has to do is to till the ground to plant the seed into the belly of the big mother and cover it. No matter what the farmer does, nature will take its time to sprout the seed. Similarly, the peasant-like initiated disciple will have to wait before seeing the birth of one's spiritual evolution. After the seed sprouts, the young plant needs care, for it is in its weakest stage of growth. Too much or too little water are both harmful to the young sapling, and therefore balance is essential. Among the deities that preside over this series of agricultural rules is Ceres. The Goddess is sometimes depicted as enthroned with baskets full of cereals around her. She symbolically represents the knowledge of agriculture, including that of harvesting, which analogically holds the knowledge of the mysteries themselves. One harvests the crop in time to have enough to sustain it during future times of need. In the same way, one gets initiated once and performs related rituals for a long time to improve one's spiritual condition. So, we do not go through dozens of initiations in a year. We usually go through one or two at most every few years. This is because a majority of our time is spent developing along the path that was opened for us during initiation. Ceres being the Godmother par excellence, the word Cereals is derived from her name. In Apuleius's mythological story of Eros and Psyche, the Goddess Ceres meets with Psyche, who is wandering in search of her husband, Eros. The girl comes by Ceres's temple and finds that the agricultural tools that are used for harvesting are scattered here and there. She takes it upon herself to collect and organize them neatly at the foot of the temple. Ceres is pleased with this, thanks her for the good work, and sends her off to meet with Goddess Juno.

Saturn, just like Ceres, has the scythe, the tool that he uses for harvesting the crops and also for ending the life of men and thus marking time in his own way. He is precisely that crescent moon that marks the birth and the death of the living world. Latent in all of us, the wisdom of Saturn is the first to awaken when we find the **lapis niger**. To work on this, he gives us the necessary tools and the time. We solve his mystery by working this mysterious stone, which like the fruit of a tree, ripens at the appropriate time with the right light of wisdom and care. We must pay close attention to Saturn's myth, the Cronos who devours his children. The practitioner risks being eaten by his own materialistic desires that is, by Saturn, but by using intelligence, he'll find a way out. By understanding the myth of Saturn, we know that we must trick him, just like how Gaia, the Mother Earth, did once. We will let him eat the black stone wrapped in swaddling in order to save Jupiter. Jupiter is the king of all those Gods who Cronos had eaten. They were waiting for a savior to free them from the womb of materialism that had consumed them. Only that sweet and beautiful Goddess that responds to the name of Juno is entitled to take care of the growth of Jupiter Optimus Maximus. She is the one who gave him to the goat Amantea, to be fed by her sacred milk. Juno Lucina, whose name means "she who brings light" was the first of the Gods to bring the light of hope, guarding that divine child Jupiter, who saved them all from the terrifying reign of the sovereign Cronos, dethroning him and taking his place. After the ascent of Jupiter to the throne, Saturn fled emasculated by his son, but from his seed, the Goddess of beauty, Venus, mother of Love, was born.[59]

We need to understand the importance of Saturn beyond this myth. Giuliano Kremmerz says that our higher psychic capabilities constantly attempt to overcome our basic animal instincts. The latter is Saturn's domain, while the psychic capabilities are managed by the Sun. These two forces and these two planets exist in opposition to each other. When winter approaches in December, Saturn reigns undeterred in the skies, and the Romans dedicate the holidays to commemorate his power in this month; but when the Sun resumes its primacy after the spring equinox, at the time of its rebirth in Aries, the court of the sky at dawn awaits the rise of our psychic consciousness. The time of Saturn is now past, and therefore he does not interfere with the powerful active force of the Sun. This is why this period is sacred because at this time, Minerva, a conscientious intelligence, is born from the head of Jupiter. Saturn reigns supreme from the 17th to 23rd December. During this time, the planet shines in the sky more than usual, and we honor his kingdom just as our sacred Roman ancestors, of great virtue, did two thousand years ago. During this time, we focus on the materialistic animal side of ourselves. There is feasting in the family and abundant nourishing of the physical body, also known in hermetic doctrines as Saturn or Earth. Moreover, since Saturn is also an opponent of Jupiter,[60] he is opposed to civil laws. In Roman times, gambling was forbidden, but it was permitted during the period of the Saturnalia, the holy December festivals dedicated to Cronos, so even today, there is a culture of playing a game of cards during these days of festivities close to the Winter Solstice. On 24th December, the day before the end of the solstice phase, the Romans, following a Chaldean tradition, celebrated the **Dies Silentii**, the Day of Silence, awaiting the rebirth of the Invigorating sun, the sun who is still young and weak, returns to lengthen the time of light over the time of darkness. The Sun, which elsewhere in the Roman Empire was celebrated as Mithras, was thus born on 25th December in a cave by a virgin as his ancient myth taught us, and which we celebrate today on Christian Christmas. Centuries, nations, and religions go by, but the truth remains.

Capitulum V
De Mytho

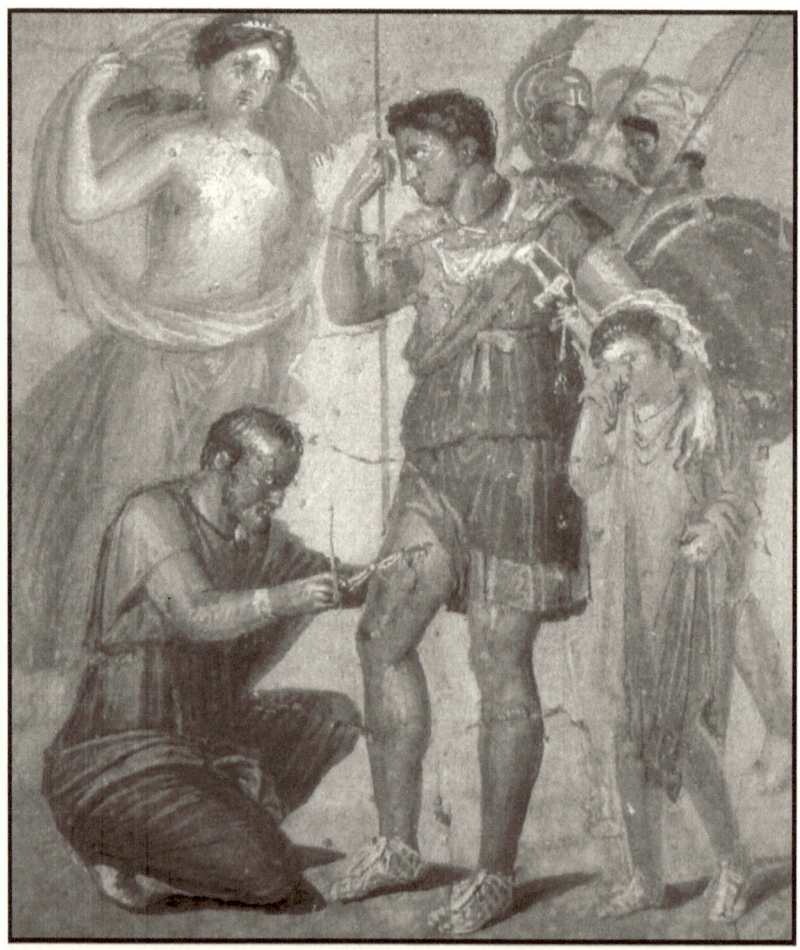

The doctor Japyx heals Aeneas (sided by his mother, Goddess Venus, and by his own son Ascanius, who is weeping), wounded on one leg. Ancient Roman fresco from the "House of Sirico" in Pompeii, Italy); mid 1st century. On display at the Museo Archeologico Nazionale (Naples).

Naples National Archaeological Museum, CC BY-SA 4.0 <https://creativecommons.org/licenses/by-sa/4.0>, via Wikimedia Commons.

Sacred Literature

The Greco-Roman mythology is probably the most important part of the sacred literature of the **Pietas**. Mythology is a literary art that not only engages both the conscious rational and the subconscious emotional natures of the people but also awakens the doors to the superconscious hermetic nature for some advanced adherents of the path. It is also a means of communication between the general practitioners and those who are the keepers of the ancient ancestral wisdom. The myths are a source of inspiration and role models for the initiates. They are a shared literary heritage that unites people from various backgrounds through symbols and stories of common origins. To this end, the Roman Republic set up a special Pontifical college with a dedicated staff of fifteen people. These fifteen were tasked with assimilating the various foreign cults into the unified state and, where possible, integrating the different beliefs into a beautiful mosaic of the Roman Spirituality. This ancient college was one of the first examples in the history of true tolerance, mutual respect, and religious integration among peoples of diverse faiths. Emperor Augustus was very dedicated to this integration. So, he tasked Virgil with writing a work that could unite the Greek tradition's sacred works such as the Iliad, the Odyssey with those of the Roman Spiritual Tradition. The main purpose behind uniting the Greek and Roman traditions was to create a common heritage with a univocal origin for all the various people living under the banner of the Roman Empire. One of the main outcomes of this project was the Roman National Epic, the Aeneid, which is considered Virgil's masterpiece. Lest one thinks that this is just an umpteenth proof that religions are created for the control of power over the people, one must know the deeper hermetic purpose behind the work of Virgil commissioned by Augustus. It is the rediscovered ordering of the symbols of the initiatory path. The ordering of the symbols should exist within the esoteric foundation of every religion so that the few can understand what for the majority is incomprehensible. In this, we can perceive the meaning of syncretism in the Roman tradition, which is always ready to receive and incorporate constructive cults. By constructive cults, we mean those ritual practices, which have a hermetic foundation to help the spiritual evolution of the individuals. Plato said that

Julius Troschel, Perseus and Andromeda, Neue Pinakothek in Munich, around 1840/50.

Rufus46, CC BY-SA 3.0 <https://creativecommons.org/licenses/by-sa/3.0>, via Wikimedia Commons.

the myth hides arcane meanings, which are not perceived by shallow people, who only see fabulous stories in them, but they are fully comprehended by those few who have the right intellect that has matured enough to grasp the underlying esoteric knowledge. With this perspective, we briefly discuss a few myths and the difficulties encountered in their interpretation in this chapter. A detailed exposition of the Greco-Roman mythology is a major research undertaking, and we will take this on in a separate work.

Perseus

The myth of Perseus seems to be very ancient and possibly has its origin from the ancient near east. It is believed that Tarsus was one of the cities in which this myth developed fully. According to some scholars, such as D. Ulansey, the cult of Perseus in Tarsus is a basic root of all the Mithraic cults that eventually spread to Rome and the rest of the Mediterranean from the first century. B.C. The myth is shaped by many components over this long journey. The Perseus cult was an initiatory cult born from the syncretism of astrological concepts and hermetic interpretations of the Perseus myth. The hero's adventures symbolize the challenges that the initiate must himself overcome. This hermetic meaning of the deeds, which are narrated in the myth, is handed down from the teacher and disclosed to the initiates during their training. Perseus was the son of Zeus, king of the Gods, and Danae, a virgin. Danae was repudiated by her father because he doubted the divine paternity of Perseus and banished them from the land. The king of Serifos, Polidette, welcomed Danae and her child, and when Perseus grew up, he entrusted him with the task of killing Medusa, the snake-haired woman who petrified anyone who looked at her. Perseus killed her with the help of his winged sandals, the helmet of Hades, which guaranteed him invisibility, and with the shining shield of Athena, which he used to dazzle the monster so as to cut off her head. From the severed head of Medusa was born Pegasus, the winged horse with which the hero saved the virgin Andromeda by defeating the sea monster to whom Andromeda was going to be offered in sacrifice to appease Poseidon.

Myth is sometimes an embellished retelling of history. Therefore, it incorporates within it not only history but other hermetic meanings. One such sacred interpretation of this myth is that it is a symbolic representation of microcosmic and macrocosmic forces that the practitioner must direct during his inner journey of knowing himself. So, the Medusa, with snakes instead of hair, is nothing but the monster of passions that lives within us, passions that must be overcome to detach ourselves from the material world. The virgin Andromeda represents the purified Soul who must be saved from the monsters of dark lust. In this way, she or symbolically the Soul can discover true love by marrying Perseus or symbolically the initiate. And, how can Perseus marry his Soul? Well, perfection is given by the hermetic androgyne, a character that contains the male and the female principle. It satisfies every need since it contains each of the two forms of the universe. So, when Perseus marries Andromeda, he reaches the purification of himself, just like another hero, Ulysses, who does the same when after his long journey, he returns to Penelope. While this is the profound, eternal, and sacred truth of the practitioners, many of the non-practitioner academic world and their cohorts in art and media, driven by ignorance and greed, make spurious interpretations of our scriptures. This is what happened recently in New York, USA, and is a poignant example of problems in myth interpretation by non-practitioners.

Problems in Myth Interpretation

On October 13, 2020, in New York, the world capital of money and media, Medusa's statue, which inverts the Perseus myth, was unveiled. The monster is not defeated by Perseus anymore, but instead, the hero is beheaded by the Gorgon! The sculptor of this sacrilegious work is an Italian-Argentinean artist of contemporary times, Luciano Garbati, who warped the Italian renaissance artist Cellini's work to celebrate the condemnation of that monster Harvey Weinstein, who was found guilty of numerous rapes. Seen from the perspective of the traditional practitioner of Roman Ethnic religion, Luciano expresses something crazy, that is, to rejoice in the punishment of a man who was a victim of his own arrogance and instincts. The ignorant sculptor sadly celebrates the image of the victory of the one who represents in the scared myths the affirmation of arrogance and basal instincts of the soul, the Medusa!

Despite this, we must admit that Garbati's Medusa is a work of art. This is indisputable. It reflects the movements of thought of the contemporary era. It technically exposes well the anatomy of a body that seeks rest after an act of effort. The evil snakes become soft hair, and sex disappears as if to mean the lost sexuality of women who have suffered abuse. The whole pose expresses the achieved satisfaction for the revenge obtained. Clearly, Garbati's work addresses a world that has lost the value of the myth. In fact, he barely knows it, and when he hears about it, he receives altered messages.

There are numerous neopagan texts written by profane authors who attempt to interpret ancient sacred works but end up with incredible blunders and distribute them as valid and acceptable theories. One among these false ideas is that many myths represent the affirmation of patriarchal societies to the detriment of previous matriarchal ones. Obviously, this strongly differs from the historical reality and the intrinsic values of the myth. The legacy of a nineteenth-century patriarchal society stems from centuries of Christianity, a religion that in imposing itself dictated new social behaviors, many of which were justified by the misogyny inherent in some of its teachings. These attitudes came into conflict with the ancient society, which gave women very different and respectable roles compared to those we are told to believe. Just think of the many female priesthoods of the ancient world, the many women poets, philosophers, and scientists, of which little is known because of a ***damnatio memoriae*** in relation to female roles applied by the new Christian societies.

Before the advent of these Christian impositions, there were no patriarchal or matriarchal societies but rather a diversity of healthy societies. The Roman society, which was one among those, was based on the value of gender complementarity. One could not live without the other, and both genders had to meet again to rediscover the androgyny of the Monad, the primordial force that gave birth to the world. The same concept of divinity in an absolute sense transcended from the simplicity of gender and ascended to the idea of androgyny. The orphic hymn dedicated to Zeus describes him as a unique deity and that each deity is a different manifestation of Zeus and that Zeus is both male and female at the same time.

Therefore, in the theology of ancient cults, there was no predominance of one gender over another instead they repeatedly talked about the coexistence and union of sexes. The cultural remnants of the ancient world, during the Christian era, are manifested in the so-called hermetic and alchemical sciences, where the goal of the "philosopher" is to return to the Monad reconquering the condition of primordial androgyny, the result of the encounter of the male with the female, the king with the Queen, the Sun with the Moon, gold with silver, or the Spirit with the Soul.

Obviously, ancient mythology was the basic theological system through which they presented many ethical teachings, which concealed important mysteries related to the spiritual realization. However, it needed a fundamental instrument, namely proper interpretation. Only through it could one understand how one should approach this knowledge and the rituals that would allow the achievement of the aspired spiritual realization. Plato gave particular importance to this instrument, defining it as useful

Benvenuto Cellini, Perseus, Loggia dei Lanzi, Florence, Italy.

JoJan, Public domain, via Wikimedia Commons.

and valid once it becomes esoteric, that is, a profound interpretation that went beyond the superficial meaning into the sacred depths of the myth.

That instrument remains very valid even today for understanding the myth and the conquest of the mysterious rites hidden in it. Unfortunately, in today's world, founded on egalitarianism, many people claim the merit of having interpreted the myth while spreading rituals that lead to cognitive-behavioral disorders in their followers. For example, some individuals have created rituals where Medusa is honored at the expense of Perseus, convinced to redeem an ancestral Mother Goddess, hidden by the catholic patriarch! No matter their intentions, how much ever they reinterpret the myth in their own way and give new and different values to those characters, the myths still maintain the original values. Therefore, those new practitioners, to the detriment of the salubrity of their own Spirit, evoke the chaotic and disorderly forces represented by Medusa. Once they so decapitate their Spirit, they will not find the purity of the Soul symbolized by Andromeda. It follows that from the execution of such invented rites, people become horribly imbalanced. Many such lost souls have come to our Temples of **Pietas** to correct their mistakes and find their balance. Getting back to the myth at hand, let us analyze the situation for a moment, to understand Luciano's interpretative error, which comes from a superficial and limited understanding of the sacred story. The main confusion stems from the wrong understanding of the clash between Perseus and Medusa. This mythical conflict is being used out of context by Luciano in his work in which he extracted, isolated, and thereby depleted the sacred myth of its depth.

Perseus represents the Spirit of the human being, which must lead the person to the attainment of wisdom, which is a blessing of Minerva, the Goddess born from the head of Jupiter. Therefore, Jupiter protects the hero, Perseus, who is in pursuit of love, the God of the origins known as **eros** of whom Plato speaks, as the one who creates order from the chaos of space and time. His target is Andromeda, the pure Soul, given to us at birth but which as we age is exposed to the passions of the world; passions represented by the sea monster to which she will be sacrificed by vulgar men who fear the sacred, should Perseus fail to save her. To perform this heroic act, Perseus must use the horse Pegasus, which can only be born from the Medusa's blood. The latter was a virgin maiden devoted to Minerva, from whom she sought wisdom. The Goddess pleased her by sending her the God Neptune, who would transmit her the knowledge of the world through an act of love. Still, the young Gorgon did not understand that all this was the result of what she had asked the Goddess and thought that everything was happening because of an illicit desire of the God of the sea, so the girl ran to the temple of Goddess Minerva, to ask her to stop the God's loving ardor. Unfortunately, this displayed hubris on the part of Medusa because without realizing it, the girl thought she knew better than the Goddess what was happening. She wanted to set one God against another, and she sinned of naivety. In fact, she had asked for wisdom, but she had the presumption to imagine how it should be acquired, and by doing so, she unconsciously placed herself above the Goddess. All this shows that Medusa had asked for the knowledge when she was not yet ready to receive it, so she was overwhelmed, and this lack of preparation was shown when the girl was afraid of Neptune.

Medusa's hubris lies in her desire to know everything instantaneously. This desire of Medusa can also sprout within any person like you or me as well. One who receives knowledge when he is not yet worthy of it and disdains it when he receives it, then he creates a complex set of wrong thoughts represented by Medusa's snakes which take the place of one's hair or the normal healthy thoughts. If through one's Spirit represented by Perseus, one cuts off Medusa's head, or in other words, these confused and poisonous thoughts, then one obtains the winged horse, which is the intellectual instrument that allows one to live a healthy **eros**. **Eros** does not signify physical sex as modern psychology teaches, but love that involves all the four bodies of the individual, the physical body, the soul, the intellectual faculties, and the spirit. Such love can make us ascend into heaven. Thanks to Pegasus, the hero's spirit can reach the chained pure soul and free it from the monster of common waters or passions. The monster can be petrified by showing the head of the decapitated Gorgon. This means that the individual who kills the passionate motions of selfish overthrow and soul confusion does not let himself be tangled by vulgar collective thoughts and avoids it from devouring his soul.

Art is the mirror of society. Therefore, Garbati's statue is a true work of art because it unconsciously represents today's society, which is chaotic, unprepared, yet aspiring for wisdom. It wants to have everything but has no patience to prepare for receiving anything. It petrifies and kills the heroes who try to behead its ignorance. It refuses sacred love. It takes refuge in the temple of wisdom, passing itself off as scientific thought without understanding true science. It continuously generates poisonous thoughts to confuse those who approach it, and it refuses to see itself in the mirror because it is afraid of its own death. The chaotic passions of modern times certainly come into conflict with a firm, healthy and respectful spirituality of the natural world. Contemporary society lives on the destruction of nature, the abuse of power, rape of the vulnerable, the protection of criminals, and anything else unjust and hides everything beneath a hypocritical veil of respectability and guarantor-justice, where the condemned are nothing more than subjects who yesterday belonged to a clique but then escaped from it, unfortunate simple scapegoats.

The myth is eternal, and today we live in the age of the Gorgon, but a Perseus guided by the divine Minerva and supported by various Gods will cut off the head of the Gorgon.

Marie-Lan Nguyen, Pelias, king of Iolcos, stops on the steps of a temple as he recognises young Jason by his missing sandal.

Naples National Archaeological Museum, Public domain, via Wikimedia Commons.

Jason and the Golden Fleece

Scholars consider the myth of Jason and the Argonauts as the most ancient Greek myth that has been handed down to us. The myth is an embellished reinterpretation of events that really happened; this phenomenon is often present in Greco-Roman myths. Poets colored the historical memory with beautiful poems to pass on arcane symbolisms to subsequent generations. The passionate plots intrigue the layperson and, at the same time, are easily perceived by the most advanced practitioners. Jason's journey is dedicated to searching for the golden fleece of a winged ram called Chrysomallos, in a place known as Colchis. Obtaining the fleece will allow the hero to redeem the throne of Iolcus from Pelias, who had mistakenly invaded it. It was a difficult task that Jason had to face with his twelve companions, a very long journey across the seas on his famous ship Argo. Beyond the difficult journey, there was the formidable task of obtaining the golden fleece of Aries, which was protected by a powerful dragon. Jason, with the help of Medea, the local princess who is in love with him, manages to complete the quest. In fact, she puts the dragon to sleep with her magical powers.

From the Perseus myth earlier in this chapter, we have understood the problems of incorrect interpretation. Let us now briefly discuss how a myth lives through new stories built upon its correct interpretation. A quest similar to that of Jason is seen in the story of St. George defeating the dragon that Merlin tames and uses to make magic in the famous saga of King Arthur. Giuliano M. Kremmerz (1861–1930) was a proponent of Hermeticism. His revolutionary approach to this subject matter can be studied in a book titled "La Scienza dei Magi." In this work, he provides instructions for the performance of the "Rite of Aries," a ritual to overcome passions and material attachments and obtain the necessary psychic enlightenment so that a practitioner's inner Sun can rise again. This rite is carried out when Sun, the supreme star, enters the sign of ram at spring equinox for a month. In this solar month, when the days begin to get longer, nature, which until then was agonized by the cold and dark winter, springs forth new life. This is also the period for this purification ritual, which shines a light on the man invaded by mental darkness. I recommend this rite to anyone who desires a spiritual ascent but has so far neglected to look in that direction out of the fear of being dazzled. The parallels to Jason's story are quite apparent in this purification rite.

Aeneid, Eclogues and Georgics

Once upon a time, there was a great **Pontifex Maximus** whose stature was augmented by his authority that came naturally to him, maybe by the omen of his birth star in Capricorn, during which the Sun is in ascendant. He honored the wisdom he was blessed with without aggrandizing himself in any way. He rejected monarchical titles and instead called himself **Princeps Civitatis** ("First Citizen") even though the Senate granted him lifetime powers of supreme military command, tribune, and censor. Everywhere he built temples to the **Numen**. Never feeding his ego, but piously giving strength and power to the Gods of his motherland so that she could be reborn from civil wars that grieved her. His name was Gaius Julius Caesar Octavian Augustus, son of the divine Julius. He established bridges between the world of mortals and that of the Gods and made sure that the virtues, which are the divine beings that must pervade amongst men, could descend from heaven to earth and incorporate into the hearts and minds of his countrymen. All recognized him as the true father of the nation who not only managed the political renaissance of his people but also of their piety, creating a new theology that brought together the peoples of the Mediterranean who lived under the common Roman insignia. The face of this new religion was Publius Vergilius Maro, author of the Aeneid, the Eclogues, and the Georgics. These books that we consider as simple writings of poetry are sacred scriptures of this great new theology.

When false convictions and impressions built in our lives are removed, there emerges a new character, that of piety, which overcomes religion's superstition. This is represented by Aeneas, who flees from Ilium, carrying on his shoulders his father Anchises and Palladium, the sacred wooden statue of Goddess Athena. Therefore, he is the man who carries on his shoulders the history and the wisdom. With him, the luminous practice begins the path for the realization that will manifest itself in the foundation of Rome, which his descendant, Romulus, accomplished. The God Mars lulled the pure soul of a descendant of our tradition's first hero's, that is Aeneas' daughter, and she gave birth to Romulus, the one who squared the four elements and became the founder of Rome, which laid the foundation for the ascent to heaven and the awakening of the seven kings or the great seven Gods [62].

In the Eclogues and the Georgics, the sacred *vate*, gives many teachings for the initiates. The greatest among those is the famous line **Omnia vincit amor, et nos cedamus amori** from the Xth Eclogues[63]. He presents the mysteries of love in a subtle way using agricultural and animal husbandry activities as metaphors. In the Georgics, he refers esoterically to the agricultural tools of the peasants as instruments that create art.[64] The plowshare and the heavy force of the curved plow, the wagons of Ceres the Eleusinian mother, the threshers and the travois, the rakes of excessive weight,[65] then again the wicker tools that Celeus learned from Ceres, the mystical sifter of Bacchus, a tool to separate the wheat from the chaff, symbol of purification in the Eleusinian rites, all hide within their descriptions many hermetical secrets. Saturn's mysteries teach us that our spiritual practice must mimic our agricultural practices and natural cycles. Just as various activities in the cultivation of crops are undertaken at appropriate times, activities in the cultivation of the divine in oneself have a schedule. Virgil poetically expresses the same message. One of the greatest teachings that Virgil gives us in these writings is the technical description of how the cycles of time are interpreted through the stars and constellations. Here is an example of the same where Virgil is esoterically explaining that when a certain star is rising, one can perform those mysterious rituals, which are symbolically portrayed in the labors of the farmers.

Virgil said, "But if it be For wheaten harvest and the hardy spelt, Thou tax the soil, to corn-ears wholly given, Let Atlas' daughters hide them in the dawn, The Cretan star, a crown of fire, depart, Or e'er the furrow's claim of seed thou quit, Or haste thee to entrust the whole year's hope. To earth that would not."

De Mytho | 111

Jean-Baptiste Wicar, Virgil reading the Aeneid to Augustus, Octavia, and Livia.

Jean-Baptiste Wicar, Public domain, via Wikimedia Commons.

Iliad and Odyssey

The Iliad and the Odyssey were the sacred books of our Greco-Roman ancestors as they are for the practitioners of the ***Pietas*** today. These texts are presented to us in schools as the stories of ancient poets, first handed down orally and then transmitted through alphabetic writing. Ancient poets sang their stories to teach and pass on esoteric doctrines. Thus, the greatest of all mysteries is treated equally by Hesiod and Homer, the ancient vati[66]. Since the day of our birth, the culture that is imposed on us, whatever it is, creates impressions and convictions in us about the world. It is easy to live thinking that the world functions as it is presented to us in school, at home, or in church. Some do try to escape from the restraints of these convictions and impressions and reach the truth, but they have some challenges to surmount. We are comprised of four levels, the physical body, intelligence, soul, and spirit. Saturn rules the physical body, which corresponds to the Earth element. The intelligence corresponds to the element Air and is in the domain of Mercury, who is the messenger of the Gods and the link between heaven and earth. The soul corresponds with the Water element and is ruled by the Moon. The spirit is ruled by the Sun and corresponds to the element Fire. To know the truth, it needs to be realized at the spirit level, and no matter how close one gets to the truth, there will still be barriers that prevent the spirit from grasping it because of the remnants of the impressions from one's past that are stored in the soul. These impressions must be eliminated from the soul, and the soul must be purified before the self can see the truth.

We can interpret the city of Troy with its inhabitants as these impressions and the convictions built in us from those impressions as the high walls of the city of Troy. The values of loyalty, conjugal fidelity, the courageous struggle for the defense of the homeland and of the family are represented by Hector, while those of deception and voluptuous pleasures are shown through Paris. Similarly, all the characters of Troy are characters can develop in us too and become various components of our ego erected on the foundation of our past impressions. The struggle of the Greeks against Troy

Johann Heinrich Wilhelm Tischbein, Odysseus and Penelope.

Johann Heinrich Wilhelm Tischbein, Public domain, via Wikimedia Commons.

represents the struggle that the individual takes on against his convictions based on past impressions that are rooted deep within his soul. In this internal battle, various kinds of personalities can manifest themselves from within the individual. Some undertake the initiatory path convinced in its efficacy to deliver them materialistic success, prove their omnipotence and demonstrate their superiority, as is the case with Agamemnon. There may be others who study and research philosophy for honor and glory, but they are destined to fail even before they conquer Troy, like Achilles son of Peleus. Then there are those who manage to conquer Troy not to seek glories, honors, or material advantages, but only for the spirit of duty towards himself and his companions. This is Ulysses, also known as Odysseus, who represents the initiate who succeeds in surmounting his past impressions and their convictions with tact. Using the Trojan horse, he defrauds his false convictions and annihilates them, thus becoming a man free from the impressions received during his life. This allows him to undertake his journey back home, to Ithaca, where Penelope with white arms, whiter than ivory or the pure soul, awaits him. Despite the Proci,[67] who symbolize evil thoughts that undermine the soul, she never gives up on the hope of meeting with her husband, the spirit. Ulysses is symbolically the Spirit that incarnates and manifests itself in the man who takes the path not for interest, not for vainglory, but for the pure love of his Soul. Until one clears his Soul of past impressions, this Spirit remains hidden to the initiate. She will go through periods of fasting and chastity tossed by the waters of the passions, and she will pass atrocious torments and will face different trials before she can reach the island of her birth. The spiritual practice will be the raft that will take her to different islands of consciousness. At the start, she will have her companions with her, but they will fail to get past the many challenges of the inner journey, and only she will succeed in returning home. Homer has described for the curious what awaits those who undertake this arduous journey back to the house of the fathers. She must choose between the two evils of Scylla and Charybdis, who fight to get her to their respective sides and are eager to tear her apart. Then there is the one-eyed giant, Polyphemus, the cyclops born from the God of Waters, Neptune, and who, like passions, will try to swallow you. Circe will try to turn the initiates into pigs with her good deeds, and the eaters of the lotus flowers will delude you to achieve realization with their practices that will only stun you with states of ecstatic mysticism.

I might be accused that I am are trying to convince you that beautiful poems with stories that describe the ignorant and superstitious sailors who believed the sea was filled with monsters are sacred scriptures. To that, I say, if you are a Christian, you should know that Christ also walked on water to avoid those monsters and that Moses opened waters of the Red Sea to guide the people of Israel, enslaved in Egypt by their passions to the promised land. I contend that there is only one message and one truth in all these doctrines. At this point, my dear reader, you might say, "So now you are mixing Ulysses and the Danai people with Moses and people of Israel, and you dare say that all these myths contain but one truth. If it is so, you need to demonstrate it. Otherwise, you will be nothing more than a scoundrel if not a charlatan!"

Oh, reader! Why are you tormenting thyself, asking me questions about the affliction of your soul? You seek answers everywhere, but wherever you go, you only smell the burning scent of sulfur and Mercury, unconsciously consumed by those religious priests who consider themselves alchemists! They forget what being an alchemist means and keep on eating the bread of Mithra, longing for eternity and bathing in the water of Orion to consecrate themselves to their Genius. They are utterly dispersed in the mental darkness of those religions only they themselves support!

Meanwhile, you, my unwary friend, are always trying to steal impiously the sacred fire of Jupiter and desecrate the truth without proper training and understanding of the necessary knowledge, just like how Prometheus gave away the fire by succumbing to his hubris without the consent of the Gods. Pure and wise men protect the mysteries in the temple, so that the ignorant or, more importantly, the evil do not abuse this sacred knowledge. No, I cannot tell you the secret of the egg, the mystery of Man, or the great arcane of the world. However, there are many references to these precious jewels in these pages you consider simple! Here is something valuable that I can give you. Perform the rituals I have provided and praise the Gods with purity and devotion, and the truth will slowly awaken in you. In this way, you will personally experience the truth without external dogmas or impositions that imprison your soul. Knock, knock again and again, and the two-faced Lord holder of the two keys will open the door for you. Janus will open the door for you, but only if you are worthy of entering that space. The same Janus reigned on the Janiculum, which was taken away from him by those foreign occupiers who stand on the slopes called the Vatican today because here stood the hill of the vaticina, unjustly replaced by a certain Peter who holds two bolts. Make a ship and set off for the eastern coasts, where the radiant Sun of intellectual and spiritual light rises. Disembark with your Achaean warriors on the beaches of Troy and prepare to attack your false beliefs. Only by destroying them can you take the path to the truth. Do not be enslaved by new concepts, do not free yourself from one false master to go and serve another, but fight within yourself for your freedom, do not remain naive but rather go, run immediately to bring down Troy. Inside, you will find your Genius, your **Penates**, and more. Pray Pallas and Mercury to give you the message of truth, but do it during Aries every morning, abstain from food coming from dead animals and sexual desire, until the Aries dies[68] to be replaced by the bull, then you will stop your prayers and await the coming of your messenger, who will make of you a gentile, freeing you from the chains of mental slavery. To honor the deities of one's kin is a spontaneous phenomenon, and when it is done, the spiritual development is faster because every folk has its own Genii.

So, I beseech you all my Roman compatriots to stop searching in the east or west for realizing your Spirit but instead without going anywhere, search within yourself that wisdom, which our great ancestors have handed down to us through their genes and with new eyes rediscover the sacred where others have only seen profane stories.

Capitulum VI
De Magia

118 | De Magia

Marie-Lan Nguyen, Magical book formed of seven pages enclosed by a cover with a veiled woman's head and a bearded man.

Baths of Diocletian, Public domain, via Wikimedia Commons.

Magic

In our society, there are different ideas about magic and its functions. Many contemporary authors define magic as dark and negative and consider it completely foreign to our tradition. A widespread misconception amongst people is that magic is conjured by certain evil, ancient, secret, and/or satanic practices. There are even strands of alleged magicians, including new followers seeking to recover the ancient Wicca, magic scholars who think they are sorcerers, and neo-pagans. We need some clarity on this subject, about which there is a serious misunderstanding because of the lack of cultural knowledge about our tradition. The destruction of our cultural heritage began with the collapse of the Roman Empire, with persecutions against the Gentiles, continued throughout the Middle Ages until the Renaissance.

Evil witches and sorcerers would be those who use different ritualistic means that could be defined as magical for their outcome, aimed to cause harm to an individual, a group, or the society as a whole. Magician, on the other hand, would be the one who works with certain practices for the common good. It is better to say that those who collect skins of certain animals following the lunar phases, those who mix incense and prepare potions, follow ancient practices of Ceres, the Magna Mater from Lydia, and not magical ones. If, however, a practice has realized what it was supposed to realize, then there has been magic, the realization of whatever the goal was, tangible or intangible. The best is not to explain because the mysteries of magic (understood as an effect and not as a religion) are kept as secrets by the priestly classes since ancient times. These were revealed only to the advanced individuals who had both the intellectual capacity and the ethical wisdom.

In ancient Rome, the deity that oversaw magic was Mercury, also known as Hermes among the Greeks and Thoth among the Egyptians. There were similar deities for this function among the other Mediterranean peoples. Who is Mercury, and why is hermetic science called such a mystery that is revealed by the God himself only to the most deserving men? We can only say that ancient Rome's hermetic knowledge corresponded to alchemy in Egypt. The coal to be turned into a diamond was the ***lapis niger***, and the whole hermetic wisdom belongs to the mysteries of Saturn, Venus, and Fortune. There is a fundamental metal in this science necessary to work on the stone, and it is sacred to the God of magic. Since the mystery cannot be taught directly, a series of syllogisms were created to explain the techniques to the adepts and to make sure these do not fall into the wrong hands, they were described as metaphors. This method was called hermetic because it pleases God Mercury, and it is suitable to pass on the teaching even through those who were not worthy to know it. It was written in such a way that, one will not understand anything if one is not ready for divine intuitions.

The Roman magisters did practice magic. We must understand that for the ancients, magic is a condition of magnetism, a magnetism that the Romans called ***venia***, which is cognate with word Venus, the name of Goddess of attraction. A closely related word is veneration, which is to be intended to attract divinities. A Roman magistrate was a magister, an individual with a magnetic generating power, legitimately conferred to him by the state. When the Roman Senate elected a dictator, he gave total powers to a single man for six months. This highly qualified individual was called ***magister populi***. He had both political and religious powers. In fact, the Roman dictator was also ***Pontifex Maximus***. He had the magnetic generating power conferred on him by the assembly of elders or the Senate, which was not only an assembly of politicians but also of men of the highest spirituality. Roman society did not distinguish between the political and the spiritual role. Instead, it required that every citizen be committed to the spiritual path. So, political positions were conferred on men who had developed great spiritual gifts. These skills were considered magical. Therefore, when he conferred the political title of Magister, he was recognized as a "materializing magician." A Magister is a magician capable of physically manifesting what is planned or needed.

Despite this, magic in Rome was forbidden for common people. But why was magic in Rome forbidden if every Roman magistrate was a magister, that is, a creator magician? We need to understand the issue in some depth. The Romans forbade black magic, which was popular among the plebes and was mainly used to put curses called **defixiones** to solve various personal grievances or problems. These **defixiones** are often found in the archaeological excavations of the necropolises. This kind of black magic was forbidden because it was considered a crime. According to the ancient Greeks and Romans, when such crimes were committed in a city, metaphysical imbalances were unleashed against the society of that place, and to reset the delicate equilibrium, punitive actions were conducted by the Goddess Nemesis that depleted the physical, intellectual, and spiritual energies of the society. The problem was that Nemesis' balance was harming the whole society and not just those who had practiced black magic.

A Roman magistrate was a man of proven spiritual values. For this, he could practice religious magic because it was taken for granted that he would not commit acts of black magic but actions of magic in favor of the state. Certainly, these permitted magics included "strong" rites, such as the evocation of all the divinities of war and the offering of his own life and his enemies for the well-being of the Roman state and the Roman people. A good example of this is the trial of Apuleius, who was accused of practicing black magic by envious enemies. He wrote his defense in his book titled "De Magia." He demonstrated in court that he was initiated into the Egyptian mysteries to practice white magic, which is aimed at good and not evil, and for this reason, he was exonerated. In Rome, the state used magical religion for social good and forbade the evil magical acts that were for personal benefits.

Capitulum VII
De Pietate Fama Societate

Pietas, from Antiquity to Today

In the last six chapters, we took a quick tour through the vast subject of what constitutes our Roman Tradition. No book can encompass this large body of knowledge, practices, and beliefs because our tradition is not bound by any book but is a collective consciousness that we have received from our ancestors. They lived this timeless tradition in the past, we are living it during our lifetimes, and it will naturally pass on to our children in the future. This book is only an introduction to this ocean of wisdom. In this final chapter, I will elaborate on two topics. First, I will cover an important subject that sheds some light on our tradition's continuity from ancient times through the dark ages to the present. Then, I will share a bit about our organization, Associazione Tradizionale *Pietas*.

The Greek-Roman tradition is often wrongly portrayed as an interrupted and non-living tradition. Over the last twenty or so years, our organization has spent considerable effort researching this topic. It is said that the fire is kept alive under the ashes. Indeed, this is true for the Roman traditional religion. Our research concludes that our tradition's eternal fire has survived in Italy in three principal ways. Firstly, through the documented wisdom of the Italian Hermeticism and Neo-Platonic academies. Secondly, via the various rituals that have survived in our society and, lastly, implicit within the tradition's classical historical, mythological, and archaeological treasures. We will discuss the last two of the three ways first and then circle back to the documented wisdom.

To understand the popular practices, a little bit of history is helpful. The edicts of the Christian emperor Theodosius condemned to death anyone who continued to practice pagan rites and refused to convert to Christianity. Violent persecutions were carried out against the Gentiles, who then had to develop the necessity to hide many ancient rituals under the veil of these new Christian practices. Those gestures that were performed in honor of the Gods before the imposition of Christianity were subsequently performed in honor of the new Christian saints, frequently invented to preserve ancient customs. Sometimes even saints with names or epithets of divinities appeared. For example, Saint Apollo and Saint Mercury. The villages and isolated places became new fortresses of the ancient tradition, where the imperial control was weaker or, in some cases, even absent. The term village in Latin is called **Pagus**, hence the word "pagans," that is "villagers," used in a derogatory sense by Christians, as if to say that people of the countryside and from small towns had remained pagans because they lacked the Christian culture available in large cities.

Orphic, Greek, Roman, Pythagorean rituals, and so on are incredibly preserved in many regions in Italy, thanks to this concealed but direct transmission from the ancient world. The **Pietas** Traditional Association is carrying out an anthropological study on a national scale, recording and mapping all those places where these rituals have been preserved to safeguard and protect them. In the absence of this effort, there is a high probability of oblivion that could come with the cultural flattening due to the plutocratic system and modern cosmopolitanism that seeks uniformity. These destructive tendencies are so unlike the ancient ethos, which preserved and defended religious and cultural diversity. The testimonies about the surviving rituals in Italy's various regions are collected and regularly published in the association's official magazine, **Pietas**. The different local groups identified by us continue to adhere to the **Pietas** traditions. We are working to coordinate all these Italian realities and preserve the wisdom that is hidden in these rituals. Often the priests of **Pietas** are initiated into the aforementioned local rituals by the legitimate representatives of those practices, thus enabling our priests to intimately understand these rituals, their immense value, and their continuity, from the ancient world to the present day.

Historical and archaeological sources are indispensable, and we are indeed lucky that these have survived the wanton destruction of our heritage. For many modern pagan aspirants, these ancient treasures are sources to derive rituals for practicing the tradition. However, for our organization, these sources confirm the authenticity of the rituals that were transmitted to us via the hermetic strands in Italy. These strands, which are based on ancient priestly wisdom, enable the scientific development of rituals for material prosperity and spiritual evolution. The old calendars, the rites handed down by Cato, the liver of Piacenza, the poems of the ancient sacerdotal colleges, and similar sources provide supporting evidence to those who have acquired the priestly wisdom from the hermetic strands. Unfortunately, they are inaccessible knowledge domains for even the most erudite in academia, mainly because they choose to stay cloistered in their ivory towers of outdated models and never attempt to enter the Italic initiate world.

The accuracy of the teachings of the hermetic and Neoplatonic Italic strands supported by the ancient literary sources provides us confidence that our reconstruction of the ancient rites does not deviate, either in logic or form, from the ancient Roman and Magna Graecia tradition. In our practice, spiritual evolution is recognizable by having lived specific experiences, which are triggered by our rituals. With the correct spiritual preparation, the proper ritual execution as per the mandated procedures carried out at the right time will always lead to verifiable results for every practitioner. Thanks to this, we have the logical foundation for developing metaphysics and associated sacred science. The priests and Pontifices of **Pietas** have lived and proved to have lived specific experiences as per this science. Because of their proven merits and virtues, they are entrusted with the complex task of maintaining the connection of our rites and teachings with the ancient sources. This ensures that the tradition can continue to be transmitted to future generations unaltered while helping us today in our efforts to transform ourselves from **homo** to **vir**.

The hermetic academies have had numerous exponents in Italy. In contemporary times the name that stands out is Giuliano Kremmerz, founder in the early 1900's C.E. of the "Schola Philosofica Hermetica Classica Italica," which itself emerged from an Egyptian Order. This, in turn, was formed at an unspecified date from previous hermetic academies and claimed to have origins directly from the ancient world. Numerous articles and texts have been published in Italy on the origins of the Egyptian order and hermetic academies. These publications have had limited circulation and controlled dissemination because of the subject's sensitive nature. This was the area of study by a group of dedicated researchers who, in the

Ignota, Giuliano Kremmerz, 1890.

Ignota, Public domain, via Wikimedia Commons

seventies, established an organization called Centro Ermetico Universale Romano, C.E.U.R. to unearth all Greco-Roman priestly cultures that survived into our present times. My father Gianfranco Barbera, who was also the teacher of the future founders of *Pietas*, joined the C.E.U.R. and, together with others, came to argue that indeed the Schola Philosofica Hermetica Classica Italica had ancient origins and started his priestly training. What is curious is that these schools already at the beginning of 1900 C.E. had, among their internal texts, references to some particular Chaldean and Egyptian deities, whose existence we came to know only after the translation of tablets found at Ebla, the city of the Ancient Near East. These tablets were discovered by the Italian archaeologist Paolo Matthiae sometime between 1960 C.E. and 1975 C.E. In 1999 C.E., and he published numerous books and articles on this subject.

I had started my undergraduate study in archaeology, and in the year 2000 C.E., I was initiated into the therapeutic school of the Schola Philosofica Hermetica Classica Italica and immediately noticed this connection. With a little more research, I found that, in addition to many Egyptian and Chaldean practices, the Schola also held rituals that referred to Roman and Greek traditions. Most of these practices were documented as being of Pythagorean origin. It was difficult to understand how it was possible to collect rites and rituals of this many traditions in a single school. The only hypothesis that could explain this was that several ancient priests must have gathered in a literary group and started an occult transmission, which would then manifest itself, over the centuries, in those numerous Italian Neoplatonist academies, which suddenly mushroomed in the period of the Italian Renaissance. This hermetic strand claimed to originate from the ancient temples of Isis in Campania, a region of southern Italy, so it was assumed that the last pagan priests of the entire nation would have gathered at these places. Moreover, they claim that their order had for centuries its reference in Piazzetta Nilo in Naples, where an ancient statue of the God Nile, the divine personification of the river Nile, is still preserved. But what were these priests supposed to be doing when they gathered in Naples of all places? And why? A little bit of history will help in uncovering this mystery.

Around the year 391 C.E., clashes developed in Alexandria between the Christians and the local Gentiles. Here, the Christian bishop Theophilus occupied some temples in Alexandria by the concession of the emperor and did everything possible to offend the religious feelings of the pagans, including exposing and ridiculing objects of worship related to the mysteries. Olympius, a priest who had trained at the Academy of Athens, moved to Alexandria to develop his studies, tried to lead the local pagans in resistance against the Theodosian edicts, which were gradually restricting the freedom of worship for the pagans. Olympius urged the Gentiles to die rather than reject their ancestral spirituality. This led to notorious clashes, which culminated in the destruction of the library and the occupation of the Serapeum by the Christians, again by the concession of the emperor. The Gentiles were forced to flee to avoid retaliation by the Christians, as it happened, for example, to Hellenistic Neoplatonist philosopher Hypatia, who parabolic monks massacred at the behest of Bishop Cyril, nephew, and successor of Theophilus.

Ancient sources inform us that Olympius, the leader of the pagan resistance in Alexandria, took refuge in Italy. We also know from historical sources that Italy's largest Alexandrian community was in Naples. We can assume that Olympius and other priests flocked here through word of mouth from acquaintances and relatives. And as it still happens today, when a revolutionary leader moves to a place, those who support his ideas reach out to him to learn about the plans and seek advice. Unfortunately, historical sources do not tell us anything about what Olympius did in Italy, nor do we have any mention of particular acts of resistance where the army had to intervene, as it happened in Alexandria. Once he landed in Italy, Olympius was probably joined by other priests and worshippers of the Gods. Based on the current state of the historical and archaeological data in our possession, we can hypothesize that Olympius took note of the impossibility of resisting the religious choices of the imperial power and that he probably suggested the creation of a secret hermetic strand to avoid the persecutions. If these hypotheses are plausible, and indeed they are logical, then this would be the missing link to understand why there were all these different practices in the strand of the so-called "Egyptian Order." Moreover, it would be clear why it was called "Egyptian Order": not so much for the type of practices within the order, but because the leadership of these priests, who gathered and hid in Naples, was entrusted to the

Egyptian Neoplatonists, who had escaped from the Serapeum of Alexandria.

Hermeticism has always had a place in Italian culture. People like Giordano Bruno, Michelangelo, Pico Della Mirandola, Plethon, and many others have frequently referred to it. Even in the twentieth century, several important people talked and researched this subject. Unfortunately, the Italian hermetic groups have often experienced turbulent moments, including internal schisms, profanations, and defamations. All through the first decade of the twenty-first century, I spent considerable time on the phenomenon of profanations, researching to understand the underlying reasons. Sadly, my conclusions are that the ancient hermetic traditions have been sullied by invented, immoral, and baseless practices of alleged masters and priests, who are since deceased. These practices have nothing to do with the ancient Greeks and Roman traditions. This had created a lot of confusion within some Italian hermetic circles, which led to further research. It was identified that these purposeful profanations were designed to defame and devalue the authentic hermetic traditions, which were gaining too much importance in certain Italian cultural movements. Our organization is founded on morally sound and ethically indisputable ancient practices and has always distanced itself from these invented rituals. Gianfranco Barbera, our spiritual teacher, always taught his students to discern good from evil, to recognize what is original from what is false.

Gianfranco Barbera was well known for his intellectual honesty and ethical integrity. So, it happened that some representatives of the Italian hermetic strands entrusted him with some practices so that he could organize this body of Roman rituals based on his experience and judgment for the benefit of the Greco-Roman hermetic community. At that time, I had just been initiated into these practices but fortunately had some early success in spiritual life. Also, some hermeticists even considered me the reincarnation of an ancient master with pontifical qualities. Maybe my father saw something of potential in me, which is why in late 2000 C.E., he delegated to me the task of studying and organizing this large body of rites. I spent several years analyzing the logic of the rites in connection with the cycles of the ancient calendars, and reconstructed the body of ritual books of the ancient Roman priests, comparing it with the sources.

I presented it to my father, who gave it to a group of advanced initiates of our tradition for practicing and documenting their experiences. This experiment's results were pleasantly surprising, which is why, after five years of experimentation, it was decided to start the Associazione Tradizionale **Pietas** as an organization for those who wanted to pursue the classical ritualistic tradition. In the next section, I will spend some time talking about the history, ideas, and works of our organization.

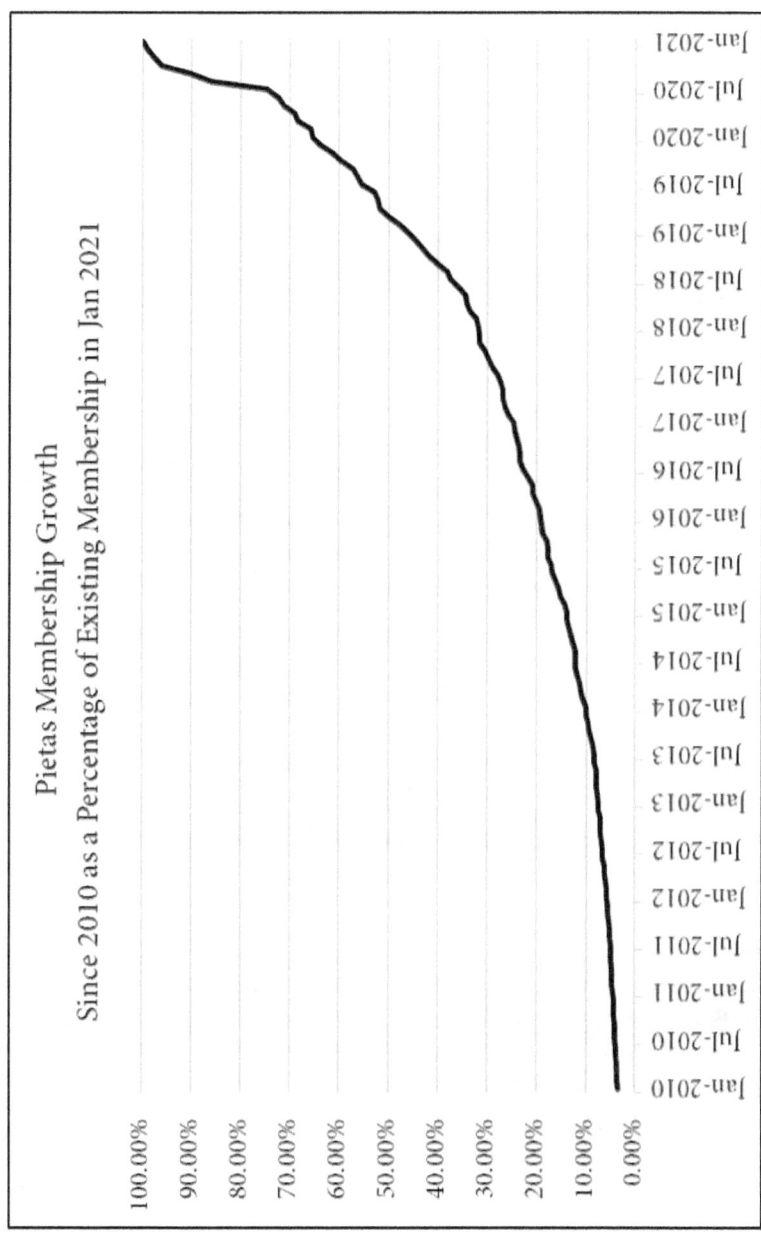

Pietas Organization

Associazione Tradizionale *Pietas* started with only six people, leaving out any form of proselytism but devoting itself more to the cultivation of the Gods and the ancient mysteries. At the end of the year 2020 C.E., *Pietas* had 320 member entities, with priests who have done at least ten years of practice, several thousand followers, seven sanctuaries in Italy with 17 temples, which receive thousands of visits every year from all over the world. Many people have felt the divine calling from the Gods and, having seen their vows fulfilled, bring gifts to these temples. Several foreign groups, officially recognized in their respective countries, have been developing direct relationships with *Pietas* for years. Given the powerful awakening of the ancient Gods, the increase in the number of followers, and the development of temples, the Spiritual Senate of *Pietas* has decided to establish a legal entity for the classical religion, called "Pietas, Gentile Community." This body organizes and manages the revival of Greco-Roman Tradition in Italy, education of the priests, and according to tradition, elaborates rituals for the contemporary age. This legal entity was founded by an official of the Italian state on December 9, 2020 C.E., 2773 years after the founding of Rome. This revival of classical religion in Italy has been very successful, and in less than a month, many people have applied for membership. Also, representatives of ethnic-religious groups from around the world are starting projects of collaboration with *Pietas*.

Technically we are two legal entities. Associazione Tradizionale *Pietas* is the cultural body and the *Pietas*-Comunità Gentile is the religious body. Both are registered in Italy and are based in Rome. Esoterically speaking, the first one represents our physical bodies and intellectual faculties, and the second our souls and spirits. We are a community of more than three hundred affiliates and partners encompassing thousands of followers who bring together people from all walks of life worldwide.

Our present organization is a successor to those groups formed by

Gianfranco Barbera, the spiritual guide of the founders of the Pietas organization.

our spiritual founder Gianfranco Barbera. He was initiated in Italian Hermeticism and introduced the same to the groups he started. From a very young age, Gianfranco sought the path of our ancestors. He never identified himself as anything else other than as a Gentile. Like Ulysses, he traveled the seas and landed at different shores until he reached the one he always longed for, the ***Via Romana***. He was the embodiment of mutual respect and dialogue. In line with the old Roman tradition, he strived to find common ground with Christianity and other religions, but over time his heart naturally abandoned this for the voice that spoke to him through his genes, the ancient Roman tradition. Even those who were ideologically opposed to him deeply respected his convictions and even commissioned him to restore their religious art in their churches. The Pythagorean philosophy and the Roman tradition are inextricably connected, and the first desire for the unity of the peninsula was born in the Crotone area based on this philosophy. Today, the city of Crotone looks like the city of Pythagoras, with its welcome signs at the entrance and monuments all through the town dedicated to the great philosopher. Before the advent of Gianfranco in Crotone, the only monument in the city was one rock placed in the center of a square in via Cutro, from which a little water gushed from time to time. The post-war sixty-year period had erased all traces of historical memory. Our founder created a cultural revolution in Crotone, raising awareness about the ancient traditions amongst the citizens regardless of their political positions. Many of Crotone's leaders had great esteem for his culture and values, so much so that they commissioned his artwork that depicts the foundation of ancient Kroton and the Pythagorean school in the hall of the provincial building on via Mario Nicoletta.

Pietas is not just a Latin word but a concept that encompasses many ideas, including the feeling of duty, the proper affection for parents, spouse, children, and friends, commitment to society, and piety through the fulfillment of the ritualistic obligation to the Gods. The word ***Pietas*** comes from the term pious, which means "pure." Originally the concept was limited to couples and described the reciprocal trust and respect between a man and his wife, but it later expanded to the relation between man and the deity. Actually, it can be called a "duty of love" because the term goes beyond respect and rises to the level of affection. For Cicero, ***Pietas*** is an act of justice as it relates to the Gods, as well as a duty (officium) and care

Gianfranco's artwork in Crotone's provincial building depicting foundation of ancient Kroton.

Gianfranco's artwork in Crotone's provincial building depicting Pythogarean school in ancient Kroton.

(cultus) for the blood relatives and finally, a duty towards the fatherland (pietas maxima). For Virgil the concept of **Pietas** also included humanitas and mercy, thus incorporating a sensitivity towards the suffering of others. The classical tradition operates based on evolution, introspection, and discovery. It is not statically fixed on itself as traditionalism can sometimes be misunderstood. It dynamically adapts to changing social conditions to shine the light of ancient wisdom thanks to the precious legacy of our ancestors, to illuminate the adherents of the path who live in today's society in a mature and modern way with intellectual honesty, equanimity, and commitment. The honesty of recognizing where the limits lie and where to seek the greatness of our tradition, giving the correct value to things and people by breaking down the bias and interests of one's ego. **Pietas** is this kind of commitment to family, friends, country, and Gods.

The Roman tradition has been persecuted, dismantled, and destroyed piece by piece. The temples were not dilapidated because they were not rebuilt but, in fact, purposefully cursed and dismantled block by block, and their splendid columns have gone to adorn, in a disharmonious way, the many churches that have arisen from their rubble. Where a temple once stood, there is always a church. In order to prevent the Roman Sacerdotes from being able to pass on their knowledge, they were persecuted and murdered. Anyone who dared to rebuild any of the temples or practice any of our ancient traditions met a similar fate. Even after the emergence of secular democracies with the separation of religion and state, there certainly has been and continues to be an effort of foreign origin aimed at keeping the Italians from their ancestral religion and culture. Probably our potential is such that others fear our domination in the event of a collective awakening of our consciousness, so they strive to keep us separate from the traditions of our homeland, to manage and control us better. Their thinking being, a rootless tree can be uprooted at any moment. They feel threatened by what is only the product of their insecurities. It took two thousand years to free us from the temporal power of this violent structure that is the Catholic Church.

Today the Italian law prohibits animal sacrifice, but it is possible to buy chickens or other animals, which are unfortunately not always certified for slaughter and consumption. Equally shameful are the inhumane industrial slaughterhouses. It must be noted that in our tradition, the humanely sacrificed animals were always eaten after the ritual, but today these rituals are banned. So sadly, the bestial acts are allowed, while the sublimation of such human rituals, to conduct the man to a higher spirituality is not. Ancient Romans had total respect for animal life. However, they were simultaneously aware of the necessity of eating meat. Faced with this, they thought of a ritual system where the citizen ate sacrificed meat. The animal to be sacrificed, had to be raised in a serene environment and sacrificed humanely only if it was led good-naturedly to the altar. In fact, the sacred law forbade the animal's sacrifice if it showed fear or anger. This is because the Roman was aware that the man feeds on the moods of the animal he eats. It is clear that a frightened and mistreated animal would have been a serious setback in the spiritual evolution of the citizen. A noble sacrifice, performed with respect for the victim, was the best way to connect spirituality with the physical need to nourish the physical body. Nowadays, the modern man is fed animals bred in fear and anger. According to the ancient dictates, the nourishment of sacrificed meat would be healthier for the soul, but that would require us to adapt our current legal system to accommodate the practices of our tradition while ensuring that we do not allow it to be misused in any way.

The same things that were done within our ancient mysteries as sacred rituals are now prohibited, but similar activities are legalized and allowed if they are experienced as the exaltation of the senses in a profane and desecrating way. This double standard should make us reflect on the total inversion of this era's values. It might seem incredible, but the tradition survived under the ashes, and now it is flourishing once again. The Gods of our ancestors always spoke and continue to speak to us, which ensured the survival of our tradition despite the cultural genocide that foreign ideologies unleashed on us for centuries. **Pietas** has taken a leadership role and is rapidly working on multiple fronts for creating the necessary physical and knowledge infrastructure to support this revolution.

The first thing that our organization is doing is building modern temples for its followers across Italy and abroad because a physical place to conduct our rituals is the core necessity for its members, and it is impractical to rebuild on the archeological ruins of the ancient sites. We are taking care that these new temples conform to our ancient scriptures. In Italy, we have built three sanctuaries in Rome. The first one is the Templum Iovis (or Sanctuarium Pietatis), the second one is the Templum Aegeria, and the third is the Templum Minervae at Olgiata. In Lazio, we have a beautiful sanctuary in Ardea, the Templum Apollinis, with basins for ablutions, bookstore, B&B, gym, rooms for banquets, conferences, and meetings. The gardens that have been designed around the temple are very well cared for and available for various community activities and rituals. In Pordenone, we built the Templum Minervae Medicae and a place for practitioners of the Triveneto. In Palermo, a sanctuary dedicated to Apollo has been built. Several more temples are being planned to be built in the coming years across Italy and abroad.

While temples provide the necessary infrastructure, it is the rituals that are at the heart of our practice. There are numerous rituals that follow our solar and lunar calendars. Some of the rituals are public, several are meant only for the followers, and others are for advanced initiates only. It takes years of research to study our scriptures and build a consensus amongst multiple interpretations of the same to come up with a practically executable ritual. A ritual must be tailored to the chosen deity, time of the year, and the purpose of the ritual. Appropriate hymns must be chosen, offerings designed, roles of various participants developed, and sequence created for executing the ritual flawlessly because the Gods are pleased when the ritual is performed with perfection. There are two projects in this area that we are working on in parallel. One, we must broaden and deepen our ritual library so that our repertoire of existing rituals continuously expands. Second, we must take our existing rituals, which we have been using over the years, and see how we can adapt them for our members around the world depending on the local conditions of those countries.

Our third front is research into the hermetic traditions of the Italian Peninsula that are based on the Pythagorean philosophy. We have set up a special purpose project called **Schola Ermetico Pitagorica Italica**. This is an important line of work for us as we comb through various available literary and archaeological resources in learning about the traditions of our ancestors. An associated project is developing an encyclopedia of historical figures, including great kings, warriors, artists, poets, and of course, those who have been instrumental in keeping the flame of our tradition alive through centuries of persecution and darkness.

Membership growth and community development is a complex challenge for any religious organization. We are open to both those whose roots trace back to the Greco-Roman tradition and those that are willing to embrace our line of thought. However, just focusing on multiplying the numbers has a detrimental impact on the organizational value system. We will all have to commit ourselves to the embodiment of the highest virtues. Otherwise, the mere attempt to meet and cooperate will be useless. The basic problem of the contemporary era is the lack of ethical values and men capable of embodying them. Rare indeed are those few who stand apart from the crowds of people that populate our country. **Pietas** is ready to give these virtuous individuals the necessary means for self-development while contributing to the collective good of our organization. While we have had a steady organic growth of our ranks, we have a long way to go with respect to proactive outreach to increase our membership. The recent official recognition as an Italian religious entity will surely help us, but most of our success will be because of our internal community-building efforts. An important thing to remember in this regard is to never act on the will of others because it would be a violation of the principle of freedom. A principle to which every individual must aspire to free himself from material chains and become eternal, but the intent of forced constraint must always be avoided out of respect for this divine strength. For us, it is important to focus on the values of the classical tradition, on the concrete results of the practice, and on the effective transformation of **homines** into **viri** – that is, from men made of mud to men made of **vis**, inner strength.

Interfaith relations based on mutual respect have always been the hallmark of Roman Tradition that sought to identify common characteristics between Roman and foreign deities to cultivate religious coexistence. In our line of work, we encounter three types of interfaith relationships. First is our relationship with organizations like us all over the world that are striving to bring back the tradition of our ancestors

Pietas Temple of Goddess Minerva in Pordenone, Italy

Pietas Temple of God Apollo in Palermo, Italy

De Pietate Fama Societate | 145

Pietas Temple of God Apollo in Ardea, Italy

Pietas Temple of God Jupiter in Rome, Italy

in a way that is meaningful to the followers of today. Around the world, various indigenous faiths are working to revive or sustain their traditions. *Pietas*' relationships with these organizations fall into the second category. Third includes relationships with the non-indigenous faiths.

For the first group, **Pietas** is always open to constructive collaboration with all the groups and/or people in Italy and abroad who want to work with us in a spirit of mutual collaboration to reestablish the traditional Roman path.

Speaking about organizations from other indigenous faiths from various countries around the world, we have strong motivations for cooperation with them. **Pietas** has very good relationships with various counterparts in Europe. We exchange ideas and provide moral support to one another as we seek to establish and grow within our respective countries. These exchanges have been extremely useful in our work. We are currently seeking to expand our relationships beyond Europe into the Americas, Australia, Asia, and Africa to develop a united nations of indigenous traditions that support each other in local, provincial, national, and international forums.

Our relationship with the first category is straight forward and the second one is both natural and mutually beneficial, but it is the third that needs some understanding. We consider non-indigenous religions as modern religions, as they have developed later, mainly over the last two millennia. Irrespective of timeline, the important thing to understand is that they have been enriched with rituals and/or theological concepts typical of ancient religions. So, despite their structural exclusivity and the history of persecutions at their hands, today, the real conflict is between tolerant factions within these religions and their extremist cousins. We look to find common ground with the tolerant factions who are open to exploring their roots, and we are always available to support them in rediscovering their ancient heritage not just in terms of knowledge but also in experiencing it through our rituals. Thanks to the presence of pro-pagan groups within modern religions, justified by their own theologies, it is possible for us to initiate and establish benevolent and mutually respectful relationships. Our spiritual founder Gianfranco Barbera was a restorer, then a lecturer at the Crotone University Consortium, who was also deeply admired by the Christian priests of the towns where he worked. They regularly commissioned restoration work and new paintings from him, both for his technical skills and for the pleasure of conversing with him about philosophy and theology, visiting him while he worked on his paintings. Even today, many churches in Calabria exhibit his works, and many Christian priests have happy memories of him, full of esteem.

The relationship of the Roman Tradition with science is an interesting one. Unlike some religions, particularly many non-indigenous ones, the classic cult has a rich tradition of science. We understand the role of science in the physical domain, but we also want to use scientific principles in understanding the metaphysical. In fact, Aristotle mentions metaphysics in his classification of scientific disciplines. Metaphysics was an essential subject of study for the ancient priests and was taught in the temples. The relationships between ritual preparation, the rite itself, and events right after the ritual are mathematical. In fact, the greatest mathematician in ancient Europe was Pythagoras, who was a Pontifex and priest. He taught that mathematics is the divine language of the Gods and Nature and can be understood through numbers. The Latin word **numerus** is composed of the root **nume**, which refers to the Latin **Numen**, and –erus has the same root of **eros**, the primordial force that turns chaos into cosmos. Therefore, numbers are the action of the love of the Numi. From here to the essence of Roman rituals, we have some numerical aspects which cannot be changed because the mathematical reality of the rite must always give a certain result. This means that the Pontifices who elaborated the rituals always kept in mind all those numbers that manifest in nature. By studying Vitruvius' "De Architectura" we find out that ancient Greeks and Romans used numbers and the numerical relationships of the human body for the design of temples, the places where rituals were performed. The Greek-Roman theology usually adapted to the scientific thought, inventions, and discoveries, and conversely, science can be found plenty within our sacred scriptures, albeit presented metaphorically. For example, if we study the latest discoveries about the birth of the universe, they match Hesiod's Theogony. The primordial chaos is described here in the same way as the modern-day understanding of singularity. The Big Bang corresponds to the action of the God Eros, who with a great warmth (moment called Eupaco) transforms the chaos/singularity into cosmic space/Uranus, where the matter/Saturn is born, which is subjected to the law of attraction/Venus. Stars and planets are created in this way, all subjected to the Cosmic Law/Jupiter. From just this simple example of the similarity between Greek-Roman Theogony and science, one can easily understand that in the classic world, there was no such thing as a distinction between the sacred and the profane or between science and **Pietas**, but both were integrated. In fact, **Pietas** encompasses all knowledge domains in one way or the other because it is a way of life. Today, the Gentile Tradition explores the ancient relationship between science and sacredness and deepens the study of metaphysics, which, just like physics, responds to precise mathematical and scientific laws. We strongly support the study of this subject to free it from the superstitious conceptions of many modern religions, which have erased and occulted it to succeed.

While we are talking about relationships, it is important to discuss media, which has always been an important part of the dissemination of information within societies, big and small. The methods and technologies that media uses have changed from ancient times to today, but the purpose and consequences of their work are still the same. **Pietas** wants to maintain a good relationship with the media sector like any other religious organization in the world. Our only complaint is that the Roman traditional religion and the Roman civilization have been portrayed incorrectly for a long time, particularly by Hollywood. We want to work closely with all media organizations and help build a better understanding within the industry about our history and traditions.

Coming to relationships with government and regulatory bodies, **Pietas** believes that modern democratic institutions and the freedom of religious practice enshrined within the laws of Italy, the E.U., and United Nations are the foundations of the modern free society. We comply with all local, provincial, national, and international laws under which our organization operates. We do not condone any forms of hate speech or illegal activities.

Pietas has come a long way since the days of its founder, and despite all the hurdles, we have been able to build a solid organization to serve our members. Our membership has steadily grown and will continue to do so. Our temple infrastructure and ritual knowledge base continue to expand. We are building strong relationships with all our stakeholders across our beloved country, Europe, and the world. We received regulatory recognition in the year 2020 of the common era, which is a great achievement not only for us but for all those on this path that for centuries have been living in the shadows. While we do not seek the full state recognition as our goal, we believe that our hard work and contribution to our society will earn us that honor as well in a few years. We believe that the Roman Spirituality has a lot to offer, and we see a bright future where, in the comity of all indigenous traditions across the world, we work for the peace and prosperity of all humanity. May all the Gods shower their blessings on everyone and help all of us to give back to the men of this era, those ethical values lost in time.

Appendices

Appendix 1: Roman Chronology

A summary of historical events of the Roman tradition from the foundation of the *Urbe* to 2020.

Period	Events
Ancient	Foundation of Rome.
I ab U.c.	
1 ab U.c.	
753 B.C.E.	
Ancient	Beginning of the Republic.
CCXLIIII ab U.c.	
244 ab U.c.	
510 B.C.E.	
Ancient	Altars of Lavinium.
CCL ab U.c.	
250 ab U.c.	
504 B.C.E.	
Ancient	Rome enters the Latin league.
CCLX ab U.c.	
260 ab U.c.	
494 B.C.E.	
Ancient	Dedication of a temple to Ceres in the Circus Maximus in Rome.
CCXL ab U.c.	
260 ab U.c.	
494 B.C.E.	
Ancient	First Roman bronze statue, dedicated to Ceres from Spurius Cassius Vecellinus. Bronze statue of the Capitoline she-wolf.
CCXLIX ab U.c.	
269 ab U.c.	
485 B.C.E.	
Ancient	Start of the war against Veio
CCCXLVII ab U.c.	
347 ab U.c.	
407 B.C.E.	

Period	Events
Ancient CCCLVII ab U.c. 357 ab U.c. 397 B.C.E.	End of the Veientina war, entry of the cult of Juno to Rome.
Ancient CCCLXIII ab U.c. 363 ab U.c. 391 B.C.E.	The Gauls sack Rome.
Ancient CCCLXXIII ab U.c. 373 ab U.c. 381 B.C.E.	The statue of Jupiter Emperor is transported from the temple of Praeneste to that on the Campidoglio.
Ancient CCCXC ca. ab U.c. 390 ab U.c. 364 B.C.E.	Erection of the so called temple C of Largo Argentina.
Ancient CDX ab U.c. 410 ab U.c. 344 B.C.E.	Early Samnite wars.
Ancient CDXIII ab U.c. 413 ab U.c. 341 B.C.E.	A bronze statue of Pythagoras is erected in the Forum.
Ancient CDXLVIII ab U.c. 448 ab U.c. 306 B.C.E.	Great bronze statue of Hercules on the Campidoglio
Ancient CDL ab U.c. 450 ab U.c. 304 B.C.E.	The Pontifex Quinctus Fabius Pictor decorates the temple of Salus.

Period	Events
Ancient CDLX ab U.c. 460 ab U.c. 294 B.C.E.	Colossal statue of Jupiter, dedicated by Spurius Carvilius Maximus after the victory over Samnites.
Ancient CDLXXI ab U.c. 471 ab U.c. 283 B.C.E.	Tarantine war.
Ancient CDLXXXI ab U.c. 481 ab U.c. 273 B.C.E.	Tarantine war. Statues with iconographic representations of the Gods are brought to Rome for the first time.
Ancient CDLXXXIX ab U.c. 489 ab U.c. 265 B.C.E.	Beginning of the first Punic war. Opposition to the bloody cults of the Punics.
Ancient DXXXV ab U.c. 535 ab U.c. 219 B.C.E.	Statue in bronze of Juno on the Aventino, dedicated to matrons.
Ancient DXXXVII ab U.c. 537 ab U.c. 217 B.C.E.	Statue in gold of the victory of the Curia, offer of embassies of Syracusans to the Romans.
Ancient DXLIV ab U.c. 544 ab U.c. 210 B.C.E.	Taranto dam. First statues in marble of the Gods in Rome.
Ancient DXLV ab U.c. 545 ab U.c. 209 B.C.E.	Bronze statue dedicated to Ceres from the builders.

Period	Events
Ancient DXLVI ab U.c. 546 ab U.c. 208 B.C.E.	Two statues of wood of cypress are dedicated to Juno Regina and brought into procession at her temple. Livius Andronīcus writes the poems (Carmi) to Juno Regina that will be sung during the procession.
Ancient DLIX ab U.c. 559 ab U.c. 195 B.C.E.	New statue of Jupiter in Campidoglio
Ancient DLXXIV ab U.c. 574 ab U.c. 180 B.C.E.	A temple to Diana and another to Juno Regina are erected.
Ancient DCVIIabU.c ab U.c. 607 ab U.c. 147 B.C.E.	End of the third Punic war. Curse on the Carthaginian soil. Greece becomes a Roman province.
Ancient DCXVII ab U.c. 617 ab U.c. 137 B.C.E.	Brutus devotes a temple to Mars.
Ancient DCXX ab U.c. 620 ab U.c. 134 B.C.E.	Gracchi reform attempts begin.
Ancient DCXLII ab U.c. 642 ab U.c. 112 B.C.E.	Giugurtina war.
Ancient DCXCIII ab U.c. 643 ab U.c. 111 B.C.E.	First triumvirate.

Period	Events
Ancient DCXCV ab U.c. 645 ab U.c. 109 B.C.E.	Campaigns of Caesar in Gaul.
Ancient DCLII ab U.c. 652 ab U.c. 102 B.C.E.	Marius stops Cimbri and Teutons.
Ancient DCLIII . ab U.c. 653 ab U.c. 101 B.C.E.	Construction of the Temple of Honor and Virtus.
Ancient DCLXIII ab U.c. 663 ab U.c. 91 B.C.E.	Beginning of Social War. First numismatic apparitions of the name Italy. Iconographic adoption of the Bull to represent Italy.
Ancient DCLXV ab U.c. 665 ab U.c. 89 B.C.E.	End of the Social War. New Italic tribes, political ascent of Sulla.
Ancient DCLXVI ab U.c. 666 ab U.c. 88 B.C.E.	Silla's expedition against Mithridates.
Ancient DCLXI ab U.c. 671 ab U.c. 83 B.C.E.	Sanctuary of Fortune Primigenae in Praeneste.
Ancient DCLXXIX ab U.c. 679 ab U.c. 75 B.C.E.	Colossal statue of Apollo erected in Campidoglio.

Appendix 1: Roman Chronology | 157

Period	Events
Ancient	Pompey definitively defeats Mithridates. Appearance of the cult of Mithras in Rome imported by Pompey's legionaries at the end of the war against the Cilician pirates. Conquest of Syria.
DCLXXXIX ab U.c.	
689 ab U.c.	
65 B.C.E.	
Ancient	Caesar Forum
DCXCIX ab U.c.	
699 ab U.c.	
55 B.C.E.	
Ancient	End of the civil war that broke out in 701. Caesar becomes a dictator for life.
DCCVIII ab U.c.	
708 ab U.c.	
46 B.C.E.	
Ancient	Caesar gets killed.
DCCIX ab U.c.	
709 ab U.c.	
45 B.C.E.	
Ancient	Apotheosis of Caesar, right after his murder.
DCCIX ab U.c.	
709 ab U.c.	
45 B.C.E.	
Ancient	Triumvirato rei publicae costituendae of Marcus Antonius, Augustus, Lepidus.
DCCX ab U.c.	
710 ab U.c.	
44 B.C.E.	
Ancient	Battle of Actium.
DCCXXII ab U.c.	
722 ab U.c.	
32 B.C.E.	
Ancient	Egypt becomes a Roman province.
DCCXXIII ab U.c.	
723 ab U.c.	
31 B.C.E.	

Period	Events
Imperial DCCXXVI ab U.c. 726 ab U.c. 28 B.C.E.	Title of Augustus to Octavian.
Imperial DCCXL ab U.c. 740 ab U.c. 14 B.C.E.	Declaration of the erection of the Ara Pacis Augustae.
Imperial DCCLX ab U.c. 760 ab U.c. 7 C.E.	Temple of the Concordia erected in the Forum.
Imperial DCCLXVII ab U.c. 767 ab U.c. 14 C.E.	Emperor Tiberius.
Imperial DCCXC ab U.c. 790 ab U.c. 37 C.E.	Emperor Caligula.
Imperial DCCXCIV ab U.c. 794 ab U.c. 41 C.E.	Emperor Tiberius Claudius Caesar Augustus. Under his reign the sacred border of the pomerium is enlarged.
Imperial DCCCIII ab U.c. 803 ab U.c. 50 C.E.	Ara Pietatis. Pythagorean Basilica of Porta Maggiore.
Imperial DCCCVII ab U.c. 807 ab U.c. 54 C.E.	Emperor Nero. Period of great popular reforms.

Appendix 1: Roman Chronology | 159

Period	Events
Imperial DCCCXXII ab U.c. 822 ab U.c. 69 C.E.	Emperor Vespasian.
Imperial DCCCXXIII ab U.c. 823 ab U.c. 70 C.E.	Conquest of Jerusalem, destruction of the temple, and relocation of the Menorah to Rome.
Imperial DCCCXXXII ab U.c. 832 ab U.c. 79 C.E.	Titus, nicknamed the delight of mankind for its high virtues becomes Emperor.
Imperial DCCCXXXIV ab U.c. 834 ab U.c. 81 C.E.	Domitianus Emperor.
Imperial DCCCXLIX ab U.c. 849 ab U.c. 96 C.E.	Nerva Emperor.
Imperial DCCCLI ab U.c. 851 ab U.c. 98 C.E.	Emperor Trajan. The empire reaches its maximum extent.
Imperial DCCCLXX ab U.c. 870 ab U.c. 117 C.E.	Emperor Hadrianus. A refined architect restores the most important temple structures and enriches them with the most precious marble in the empire. He erects the temple of Venus and Rome after having personally designed it.
Imperial DCCCLXXIV ab U.c. 874 ab U.c. 121 C.E.	The construction of the temple dedicated to Venus in Rome is initiated.

Period	Events
Imperial DCCCXCI ab U.c. 891 ab U.c. 138 C.E.	Antoninus Pius Emperor.
Imperial DCCCXCVIII ab U.c. 898 ab U.c. 145 C.E.	Temple of the Divo Hadrianus.
Imperial CMXIV ab U.c. 914 ab U.c. 161 C.E.	Marcus Aurelius Emperor.
Imperial CMLXXVIII ab U.c. 978 ab U.c. 225 C.E.	Erection of the Mithraeum of S. Prisca.
Imperial MXXI-MXXXV ab U.c. 1021 - 1035 ab U.c. 268 - 282 C.E.	The emperors Claudius Gothicus, Aurelianus and Probus strengthen the borders of the empire and the Roman religion, guaranteeing a period of prosperity and security.
Imperial MXXVII ab U.c. 1027 ab U.c. 274 C.E.	Aurelianus erects the temple of the Sol invictus in Rome.
Imperial MXXXVII ab U.c. 1037 ab U.c. 284 C.E.	Emperor Diocletianus. It will implement the reform of the tetrarchy.
Imperial MLXV ab U.c. 1065 ab U.c. 312 C.E.	Constantine usurps the throne of Maxentius and condemns Rome to ruin, declining the public Pietas.

Appendix 1: Roman Chronology | 161

Period	Events
Imperial MLXXVII ab U.c. 1077 ab U.c. 324 C.E.	Constantine makes Christianity the official religion of the empire. At Didyma the Christians sack the oracle of Apollo and torture their priests to death. Slowly the persecutions against the gentiles begin.
Imperial MLXXXIII ab U.c. 1083 ab U.c. 330 C.E.	Constantine, full of Godlessness, turns the eagle against the course of the sky and makes Constantinople capital of the Empire.
Imperial MCXIV ab U.c. 1114 ab U.c. 361 C.E.	Julian becomes emperor and puts an end to Christian persecutions against Gentiles with a new period of tolerance. Tries to recover the traditional Pietas marred by previous emperors.
Imperial MCXIX ab U.c. 1119 ab U.c. 366 C.E.	Julian dies during an expedition against the Parthians. According to some reports, he was treacherously shot behind by a Christian legionary named Mercury. He (Mercury) was soon made a saint of the Christian church.
Imperial MCXXXI ab U.c. 1131 ab U.c. 378 C.E.	Theodoric divides the empire.
Imperial MCXXXIII ab U.c. 1133 ab U.c. 380 C.E.	Theodosius outlaws the Roman tradition (!). Christians attack the temple of Eleusis. The Hierophant Nestorius puts an end to the Eleusinian mysteries and announces the predominance of mental darkness over the human race.
Imperial MCLIX ab U.c. 1159 ab U.c. 406 C.E.	The inability of the Christian emperors to defend the borders of the empire leads to severe barbaric infiltrations across the Rhine.
Imperial MCCXXIX ab U.c. 1229 ab U.c. 476 C.E.	Romolus Augustulus is deposed. The Western Roman Empire ends due to the loss of Pietas.

Appendix 1: Roman Chronology

Period	Events
Medivial MCCLXXX ab U.c. 1280 ab U.c. 527 C.E.	Justinian Emperor of the East tries to recover part of the ancient Roman values and regain some territories in Italy.
Medivial MDLIII ab U.c. 1553 ab U.c. 800 C.E.	Emperor Charlemagne of the Holy Roman Empire, a vain emulation of the ancient Roman empire.
Medivial MDXCVI ab U.c. 1596 ab U.c. 843 C.E.	The Carolingian empire.
Medivial MCMV ab U.c. 1905 ab U.c. 1152 C.E.	Frederick I restores the Holy Roman Empire.
Medivial MCMXLVII ab U.c. 1947 ab U.c. 1194 C.E.	Henry VI joins the Kingdom of Sicily to the sacred Roman Empire.
Medivial MCMLXXIII ab U.c. 1973 ab U.c. 1220 C.E.	Frederick II of Swabia emperor of the Holy Roman Empire. He moves the headquarters to Italy, subjugates the municipalities and starts a policy against the state of the church. Hermetic scholar made his kingdom a glimmer of light in the dark of the Middle Ages.
Medivial MMCCVI ab U.c. 2206 ab U.c. 1453 C.E.	The Turks conquer Constantinople. Half a century before the modern era the last bastion of the Roman world collapses, now deprived of its virtue for centuries due to the lack of Pietas.
Dark MMCCVII-MMDCCXV ab U.c. 2207 - 2713 ab U.c. 1454 - 1960 C.E.	Secret practice of Pietas across the former Roman Empire.

Appendix 1: Roman Chronology | 163

Period	Events
Contemporary MMDCCXIV ab U.c. 2714 ab U.c. 1961 C.E.	Gianfranco Barbera realizes the terracotta mask that one day will dominate the sanctuary of the Pietas.
Contemporary MMDCCLVIII ab U.c. 2758 ab U.c. 2005 C.E.	On January the 5th, Giuseppe Barbera founds the Pietas Traditional Association in Italy.
Contemporary MMDCCLX ab U.c. 2760 ab U.c. 2007 C.E.	The Aedes Romae Pietatis is founded in Rome, the first Gentile temple in Italy.
Contemporary MMDCCLX ab U.c. 2760 ab U.c. 2007 C.E.	Pietas magazine is born.
Contemporary MMDCCLXI ab U.c. 2761 ab U.c. 2008 C.E.	The small church of the Gragna of Gagliato (CZ), in southern Italy, which stood on an ancient solar temple, is converted into a temple dedicated to Apollo.
Contemporary MMDCCLXI ab U.c. 2761 ab U.c. 2008 C.E.	The first national camp of the Roman-Italic traditionalists (Campo di Flora) is held in Chiaravalle Centrale, in Calabria, in southern Italy.
Contemporary MMDCCLXII ab U.c. 2762 ab U.c. 2009 C.E.	The Templum Minervae is opened in Rome (La Storta district), which in 2010 of the common era will host the World Congress of Ethnic Religions (WCER).
Contemporary MMDCCLXV ab U.c. 2765 ab U.c. 2012 C.E.	The Sanctuarium Pietatis is founded in Rome on July the 13th, where the Aedes Romae Pietatis is transferred and consecrated the 12th of December 2012 of the Common Era.

Period	Events
Contemporary MMDCCLXVI ab U.c. 2766 ab U.c. 2013 C.E.	On April 21, the Sanctuarium Pietatis hosts the first international conference on Greek-Roman Tradition: here come delegations from the YSEE of Vlassis Rassias and the Thyrsos group. The latter proposed the flag of Julian as a symbol of brotherhood between the Greek and Roman groups. An active collaboration is started today.
Contemporary MMDCCLXX ab U.c. 2770 ab U.c. 2017 C.E.	In June the Temple of Jupiter is consecrated and opened to the public, in the Sanctuarium Pietatis of Rome.
Contemporary MMDCCLXXI ab U.c. 2771 ab U.c. 2018 C.E.	In April, a YSEE delegation with Vlassis Rassias comes to visit the temple of Jupiter in Rome, to honor the erection of the temple.
Contemporary MMDCCLXXI ab U.c. 2771 ab U.c. 2018 C.E.	On June the 21st, a Pietas delegation is hosted by the Greek groups Thyrsos and YSEE at the summer solstice celebrations. Pietas and Thyrsos reaffirm the bond of international brotherhood and exchange flags with the effigy that was chosen by the emperor Julian.
Contemporary MMDCCLXXI ab U.c. 2771 ab U.c. 2018 C.E.	In August, a temple dedicated to Minerva Medica, the first therapeutic temple of the contemporary era, was erected in Fiumefreddo (PD) in northern Italy in just four days.
Contemporary MMDCCLXXI ab U.c. 2771 ab U.c. 2018 C.E.	In December, the temple of Apollo in Ardea was erected and consecrated.
Contemporary MMDCCLXXII ab U.c. 2772 ab U.c. 2019 C.E.	The temple of Minerva in Rome (La Storta) is moved to a larger location in the neighborhood of Olgiata.

Period	Events
Contemporary MMDCCLXXIII ab U.c. 2773 ab U.c. 2020 C.E.	On July 11th, foundation of the temple of Apollo in Sicily in the city of Palermo.
Contemporary MMDCCLXXIII ab U.c. 2773 ab U.c. 2020 C.E.	On July 13th, a temple was erected and consecrated to Apollo Pizio Iperboreo in the Sanctuarium Pietatis of Rome.
Contemporary MMDCCLXXIII ab U.c. 2773 ab U.c. 2020 C.E.	On December 9th, official foundation of the juridical body for the Gentile religion in Italy named Pietas - Gentile Community

Appendix 2: *Pietas* Calendar

The Kalendarium is the eternal repetition of the myth, and through it the Roman man brings into harmony the Gods of his inner microcosm with the greater macrocosm. Based on astronomy and astrology, the Roman calendar has changed several times and guided the various Pontifices throughout history. Here in this appendix, we have the calendar of our rituals for the year 2021 of the common era. It should be noted that among the private rituaria some change according to the lunar phases as opposed to a given calendar day in the common era month. For example, **Kalendae**, **Nonae** and **Idus** correspond to the New Moon, First Quarter Moon, and Full Moon respectively. So, every year, the Pontifex Maximus of *Pietas* generates a customized Kalendarium for that year for the community indicating on it the corresponding solar calendar dates for these lunar based rituals. Another important aspect in this regard to know is that the Holy Roman year begins in March on the day of Vernal Equinox, when nature returns lush and the day and night are in perfect equilibrium. This month is dedicated to God Mars, father of Romulus, the sacred sovereign.

Some cautionary guidance is necessary here given that many may attempt to use this calendar to do these rituals on their own. The Roman domestic rituaria, apart from specific exceptions, takes place only in the morning, at its **Lararium**, which is a small temple in the house of the adherent. Here the images of the deities worshiped in that family (Gens) are kept. The temple includes the **bullae** (talismans and sacred items that are worn on the body) and their own little image (Virgulto). The offers consist of fumigations of incense, fruits, vegetables, flowers, cakes, wine and special foods. These rituals are performed according to the teachings of the special priests. Those who want to practice the calendar on their own can do so as long as they follow certain necessary religious guidelines. For example, one should not approach the altars after consumption of food or indulgence in sexual pleasures. It is not that these basic human instincts are forbidden but because it is crucial to have moderation and balance, which are the most important attributes of God Jupiter. The Associazione Tradizionale *Pietas* is always available to help anyone in understanding the calendar and/or conducting these rituals. You can reach us via our website at https://tradizioneromana.org or via our facebook page at https://www.facebook.com/AssociazioneTradizionalePietas.

2021 Equinoxes and Solstices		
Event	Date	Solar Zodiac
Spring Equinox	21-Mar-21 10:38	Sun in Aries
Summer Solstice	21-Jun-21 04:31	Sun in Cancer
Autumn Equinox	22-Sep-21 20:20	Sun in Libra
Winter Solstice	21-Dec-21 16:56	Sun in Capricon

2021 Eclipses		
Eclipse	Date Time	Visible in Italy
Lunar	26-May-21 12:15	No
Solar	06-Oct-21 11:44	Yes
Lunar	19-Nov-21 10:05	No
Solar	04-Dec-21 08:32	Yes

2021 New Moon and Kalendae Ritual Dates		
Lunar Month	New Moon	Kalendae
January	13-Jan-21 06:03	13-Jan-21
February	11-Feb-21 20:08	12-Feb-21
March	13-Mar-21 11:24	13-Mar-21
April	12-Apr-21 03:33	12-Apr-21
May	11-May-21 20:02	11-May-21
June	10-Jun-21 11:54	10-Jun-21
July	10-Jul-21 02:18	10-Jul-21
August	08-Aug-21 14:51	09-Aug-21
September	07-Sep-21 01:52	07-Sep-21
October	06-Oct-21 12:06	06-Oct-21
November	04-Nov-21 22:15	05-Nov-21
December	04-Dec-21 08:45	04-Dec-21

2021 First Quarter and Nonae Ritual Dates

Lunar Month	First Quarter	Nonae
January	20-Jan-21 22:04	21-Jan-21
February	19-Feb-21 19:49	20-Feb-21
March	21-Mar-21 15:42	22-Mar-21
April	20-Apr-21 08:00	20-Apr-21
May	19-May-21 20:13	20-May-21
June	18-Jun-21 04:55	18-Jun-21
July	17-Jul-21 11:12	17-Jul-21
August	15-Aug-21 16:21	16-Aug-21
September	13-Sep-21 21:41	14-Sep-21
October	13-Oct-21 04:28	13-Oct-21
November	11-Nov-21 13:48	12-Nov-21
December	11-Dec-21 02:38	11-Dec-21

2021 Full Moon and Idus Ritual Dates

Lunar Month	Full Moon	Idus
January	28-Jan-21 20:19	29-Jan-21
February	27-Feb-21 09:20	27-Feb-21
March	28-Mar-21 19:50	29-Mar-21
April	27-Apr-21 04:33	27-Apr-21
May	26-May-21 12:15	26-May-21
June	24-Jun-21 19:40	25-Jun-21
July	24-Jul-21 03:37	24-Jul-21
August	22-Aug-21 13:02	22-Aug-21
September	21-Sep-21 00:55	21-Sep-21
October	20-Oct-21 15:58	21-Oct-21
November	19-Nov-21 10:00	19-Nov-21
December	19-Dec-21 05:38	19-Dec-21

Appendix 2: Pietas Calendar | 169

2021 January				
Day	Deity	Weekday	Solar Calendar	Lunar Calendar
1	Venus	Friday	Kalendae	
2	Saturn	Saturday		
3	Moon	Sunday	Compitalia	
4	Mars	Monday	Compitalia	
5	Mars	Tuesday	Nonae, Compitalia	
6	Mercury	Wednesday		
7	Jupiter	Thursday		
8	Venus	Friday		
9	Saturn	Saturday	Agonalia	Aganolia
10	Moon	Sunday		
11	Mars	Monday	Carmentalia	
12	Mars	Tuesday		
13	Mercury	Wednesday	Idus	(New Moon 06:03), Kalendae
14	Jupiter	Thursday		Dies Religiosus
15	Venus	Friday	Carmentalia	
16	Saturn	Saturday		
17	Moon	Sunday	Ludi Palatini	
18	Mars	Monday		
19	Mars	Tuesday		Compitalia
20	Mercury	Wednesday		(First Quarter 22:04), Compitalia
21	Jupiter	Thursday		Nonae, Compitalia
22	Venus	Friday		Dies Religiosus
23	Saturn	Saturday		
24	Moon	Sunday	Ferae Sementivae	
25	Mars	Monday	Ferae Sementivae	
26	Mars	Tuesday	Ferae Sementivae	
27	Mercury	Wednesday		
28	Jupiter	Thursday	Paganalia	Paganalia, Full Moon (20:19)
29	Venus	Friday		Idus, Ianuariae
30	Saturn	Saturday		Dies Religiosus

2021 January

Day	Deity	Weekday	Solar Calendar	Lunar Calendar
31	Moon	Sunday		

2021 February

Day	Deity	Weekday	Solar Calendar	Lunar Calendar
1	Moon	Monday	Kalendae	
2	Mars	Tuesday		
3	Mercury	Wednesday		
4	Jupiter	Thursday		
5	Venus	Friday	Nonae	
6	Saturn	Saturday		
7	Sun	Sunday		
8	Moon	Monday		
9	Mars	Tuesday		
10	Mercury	Wednesday		
11	Jupiter	Thursday	Mani Familiari	(New Moon 20:08)
12	Venus	Friday	Mani Familiari	Kalendae
13	Saturn	Saturday	Idus, Fornacalia, Virgo Vesta, Parentalia, Mani Familiari	Virgo Vesta
14	Sun	Sunday	Mani Familiari	
15	Moon	Monday	Lupercalia, Mani Familiari	
16	Mars	Tuesday	Mani Familiari	
17	Mercury	Wednesday	Quirinalia, Mani Familiari	Quirinalia
18	Jupiter	Thursday	Mani Familiari	
19	Venus	Friday	Mani Familiari	(First Quarter 19:49)
20	Saturn	Saturday	Mani Familiari	Nonae
21	Sun	Sunday	Feralia, Mani Familiari	Feralia
22	Moon	Monday	Caristia	Carista (Celebration dedicated to family love, presents between the partners)
23	Mars	Tuesday	Terminalia	Lares Familiares

Appendix 2: Pietas Calendar | 171

2021 February				
Day	Deity	Weekday	Solar Calendar	Lunar Calendar
24	Mercury	Wednesday	Regfugium	
25	Jupiter	Thursday		
26	Venus	Friday		
27	Saturn	Saturday	Equirria	Idus, Full Moon (()9:20)
28	Sun	Sunday		Dies Religiosus

2021 March				
Day	Deity	Weekday	Solar Calendar	Lunar Calendar
1	Moon	Monday	Kalendae	
2	Mars	Tuesday		
3	Mercury	Wednesday		
4	Jupiter	Thursday		
5	Venus	Friday		
6	Saturn	Saturday		
7	Sun	Sunday	Nonae	
8	Moon	Monday		
9	Mars	Tuesday		
10	Mercury	Wednesday		
11	Jupiter	Thursday		Equirria
12	Venus	Friday		
13	Saturn	Saturday		Kalendae (New Moon11:24)
14	Sun	Sunday	Equirria	Dies Religiosus
15	Moon	Monday	Idvs	
16	Mars	Tuesday	Mani Familiari	
17	Mercury	Wednesday	Liberalia	Liber
18	Jupiter	Thursday		
19	Venus	Friday	Quinquatrus Minervalia	Minerva
20	Saturn	Saturday	Sun in Aries - 10:38	
21	Sun	Sunday		First quarter 15:42

2021 March

Day	Deity	Weekday	Solar Calendar	Lunar Calendar
22	Moon	Monday		Nonae
23	Mars	Tuesday	Tubilustrium	Tubilustrium
24	Mercury	Wednesday	Q.REX.C.F.	
25	Jupiter	Thursday		
26	Venus	Friday		
27	Saturn	Saturday		
28	Sun	Sunday	Daylight savings time	Equirria (Full Moon 19:50)
29	Moon	Monday		Idvs
30	Mars	Tuesday		Dies Religiosus
31	Mercury	Wednesday		

2021 April

Day	Deity	Weekday	Solar Calendar	Lunar Calendar
1	Jupiter	Thursday	Kalendae	
2	Venus	Friday		
3	Saturn	Saturday		
4	Sun	Sunday		
5	Moon	Monday	Nonae	
6	Mars	Tuesday		
7	Mercury	Wednesday		
8	Jupiter	Thursday		Castoress Dies Natalis
9	Venus	Friday		Dies Religiosus
10	Saturn	Saturday		
11	Sun	Sunday		Diana
12	Moon	Monday		Kalendae (New Moon 03:33)
13	Mars	Tuesday	Idvs	Dies Religiosus
14	Mercury	Wednesday		
15	Jupiter	Thursday	Fordicidia	
16	Venus	Friday		
17	Saturn	Saturday		

Appendix 2: Pietas Calendar | 173

2021 April

Day	Deity	Weekday	Solar Calendar	Lunar Calendar
18	Sun	Sunday		
19	Moon	Monday	Cerealia	
20	Mars	Tuesday		Nonae (First quarter 08:00)
21	Mercury	Wednesday	Parilia	Dies Natalis Romae
22	Jupiter	Thursday	Dies Natalies Vlassis Rassias	
23	Venus	Friday	Vinalia	Venere Ericina - Vinalia
24	Saturn	Saturday		
25	Sun	Sunday	Robigalia	
26	Moon	Monday		
27	Mars	Tuesday		Idus (Full Moon 19:50)
28	Mercury	Wednesday	Floralia	Floralia
29	Jupiter	Thursday	Floralia	Floralia
30	Venus	Friday	Floralia	Floralia

2021 May

Day	Deity	Weekday	Solar Calendar	Lunar Calendar
1	Saturn	Saturday	Kalendae Floralia	Floralia
2	Sun	Sunday	Floralia	Floralia
3	Moon	Monday	Floralia	Floralia
4	Mars	Tuesday		
5	Mercury	Wednesday		
6	Jupiter	Thursday		
7	Venus	Friday	Nonae	
8	Saturn	Saturday		
9	Sun	Sunday	Lemuria	
10	Moon	Monday		
11	Mars	Tuesday	Lemuria	New Moon 20:02
12	Mercury	Wednesday		Kalendae Maiae
13	Jupiter	Thursday	Lemuria	Lemuria

2021 May				
Day	Deity	Weekday	Solar Calendar	Lunar Calendar
14	Venus	Friday		
15	Saturn	Saturday	Idvs	
16	Sun	Sunday		
17	Moon	Monday		
18	Mars	Tuesday		
19	Mercury	Wednesday		First quarter 20:13
20	Jupiter	Thursday		Nonae Natalis Apollinis
21	Venus	Friday	Agonalia	Iano
22	Saturn	Saturday		
23	Sun	Sunday	Tubilustrium	
24	Moon	Monday	Q.REX.C.F.	
25	Mars	Tuesday		
26	Mercury	Wednesday		Idvs (Full Moon 12:!5)
27	Jupiter	Thursday		Dies Religiosus
28	Venus	Friday		
29	Saturn	Saturday	Ambarvalia	
30	Sun	Sunday		
31	Moon	Monday		

2021 June				
Day	Deity	Weekday	Solar Calendar	Lunar Calendar
1	Mars	Tuesday	Kalendae	
2	Mercury	Wednesday		
3	Jupiter	Thursday		
4	Venus	Friday		
5	Saturn	Saturday	Nonae	
6	Sun	Sunday		
7	Moon	Monday		
8	Mars	Tuesday	Mens	Mens
9	Mercury	Wednesday	Vestalia	Vestalia

2021 June

Day	Deity	Weekday	Solar Calendar	Lunar Calendar
10	Jupiter	Thursday		Kalendae Virile (New Moon 11:54)
11	Venus	Friday	Matralia	Mater Matuta - Fortuna - Concordia
12	Saturn	Saturday		
13	Sun	Sunday	Idvs	
14	Moon	Monday		
15	Mars	Tuesday	Q. STERCUS. D. F.	Q.S.D.F.
16	Mercury	Wednesday		
17	Jupiter	Thursday		
18	Venus	Friday		Nonae (First Quarter 04:55)
19	Saturn	Saturday		Dies Religiosus
20	Sun	Sunday		
21	Moon	Monday	Sun in Cancer - 04:21	Apollo Catartico
22	Mars	Tuesday		
23	Mercury	Wednesday		
24	Jupiter	Thursday		Fors Fortunae (Full Moon 19:40)
25	Venus	Friday		Idvs
26	Saturn	Saturday		Dies Religiosus
27	Sun	Sunday		
28	Moon	Monday		
29	Mars	Tuesday		
30	Mercury	Wednesday		

2021 July

Day	Deity	Weekday	Solar Calendar	Lunar Calendar
1	Jupiter	Thursday	Kalendae	
2	Venus	Friday		
3	Saturn	Saturday		
4	Sun	Sunday		

2021 July				
Day	Deity	Weekday	Solar Calendar	Lunar Calendar
5	Moon	Monday	Poplifugia	
6	Mars	Tuesday	Ludi Apollinaris	Fortuna Muliebre
7	Mercury	Wednesday	Nonae - Commemoration V.R.	
8	Jupiter	Thursday		
9	Venus	Friday		
10	Saturn	Saturday		Kalendae (New Moon 02:18)
11	Sun	Sunday		Dies Religiosus
12	Moon	Monday		
13	Mars	Tuesday	Apollo	Apollo
14	Mercury	Wednesday		
15	Jupiter	Thursday	Idvs	
16	Venus	Friday		
17	Saturn	Saturday		Nonae (First Quarter 11:12)
18	Sun	Sunday		Dies Religiosus
19	Moon	Monday	Lucaria	Lucaria
20	Mars	Tuesday		
21	Mercury	Wednesday	Lucaria	Lucaria
22	Jupiter	Thursday		
23	Venus	Friday	Neptunalia	Neptunalia
24	Saturn	Saturday		Idvs (Full Moon 03:37)
25	Sun	Sunday	Furrinalia	
26	Moon	Monday		
27	Mars	Tuesday		
28	Mercury	Wednesday		
29	Jupiter	Thursday		
30	Venus	Friday		
31	Saturn	Saturday		

Appendix 2: Pietas Calendar | 177

2021 August				
Day	Deity	Weekday	Solar Calendar	Lunar Calendar
1	Sun	Sunday	Kalendae	
2	Moon	Monday		
3	Mars	Tuesday		
4	Mercury	Wednesday		
5	Jupiter	Thursday	Nonae	
6	Venus	Friday		
7	Saturn	Saturday		
8	Sun	Sunday		New Moon 14:51
9	Moon	Monday	Sol Indiges	Kalendae Sol Indiges
10	Mars	Tuesday		Dies Religiosus
11	Mercury	Wednesday		
12	Jupiter	Thursday	Hercvles Victor	Hercvles Victor
13	Venus	Friday	Idvs	
14	Saturn	Saturday		
15	Sun	Sunday		First Quarter 16:21
16	Moon	Monday		Nonae
17	Mars	Tuesday	Portunalia	Dies Religiosus
18	Mercury	Wednesday		
19	Jupiter	Thursday	Vinalia Rustica	
20	Venus	Friday		
21	Saturn	Saturday	Consualia	
22	Sun	Sunday		Full Moon 13:02
23	Moon	Monday	Volcanalia	Idvs
24	Mars	Tuesday	Mundus Patet	Mundus Patet
25	Mercury	Wednesday	Opi Consivia	
26	Jupiter	Thursday		
27	Venus	Friday	Volturnalia	
28	Saturn	Saturday		
29	Sun	Sunday		
30	Moon	Monday		
31	Mars	Tuesday		

2021 September

Day	Deity	Weekday	Solar Calendar	Lunar Calendar
1	Mercury	Wednesday	Kalendae	
2	Jupiter	Thursday	Feriae ex s c quod eo die imp caes divi f aug apud actium vicit	
3	Venus	Friday	F ex s c quod eo die imp caes divi f aug vicit in sicilia	
4	Saturn	Saturday	Ludi Romani	
5	Sun	Sunday		
6	Moon	Monday		
7	Mars	Tuesday		Kalendae (New Moon 01:52)
8	Mercury	Wednesday	Natalis Aureliani	Dies Religiosus
9	Jupiter	Thursday		
10	Venus	Friday		
11	Saturn	Saturday	Templum aesculapii dedicatum es	
12	Sun	Sunday		
13	Moon	Monday	Idvs	First Quarter 21:41
14	Mars	Tuesday		Nonae Sept.
15	Mercury	Wednesday		Dies Religiosus
16	Jupiter	Thursday		
17	Venus	Friday		
18	Saturn	Saturday	Natalis Traiani	
19	Sun	Sunday	Natalis Pii Antonini	
20	Moon	Monday	Natalis Romuli	
21	Mars	Tuesday		Idvs (Full Moon 00:55)
22	Mercury	Wednesday	Autumn Equinox 20:20 - Sun in Libra	Dies Religiosus
23	Jupiter	Thursday		
24	Venus	Friday		
25	Saturn	Saturday		
26	Sun	Sunday	Venus Genitrix	Venus Genitrix
27	Moon	Monday		
28	Mars	Tuesday		

Appendix 2: Pietas Calendar | 179

2021 September				
Day	Deity	Weekday	Solar Calendar	Lunar Calendar
29	Mercury	Wednesday		
30	Jupiter	Thursday		

2021 October				
Day	Deity	Weekday	Solar Calendar	Lunar Calendar
1	Venus	Friday	Kalendae	
2	Saturn	Saturday		
3	Sun	Sunday		
4	Moon	Monday	Ieiunum Cereris	
5	Mars	Tuesday	Mundus Patet	
6	Mercury	Wednesday		Kalendae (New Moon 12:06)
7	Jupiter	Thursday	Nonae	Dies Religiosus
8	Venus	Friday		
9	Saturn	Saturday	Genio Publico P.Q.R.	Genio Publico P.Q.R. Ieiunum Cereris
10	Sun	Sunday		Mundus Patet
11	Moon	Monday	Meditrinalia	Meditrinalia
12	Mars	Tuesday	Augustalia	
13	Mercury	Wednesday	Fontinalia	Nonae (First Quarter 04:28)
14	Jupiter	Thursday		Dies Religiosus
15	Venus	Friday	Idvs Eq. Oct.	
16	Saturn	Saturday		
17	Sun	Sunday		
18	Moon	Monday		
19	Mars	Tuesday	Armilustrium	
20	Mercury	Wednesday		Full Moon 15:58
21	Jupiter	Thursday		Idvs
22	Venus	Friday		Dies Religiosus
23	Saturn	Saturday		
24	Sun	Sunday	Favor-Venus Ericina	Favor-Venus Ericina

2021 October

Day	Deity	Weekday	Solar Calendar	Lunar Calendar
25	Moon	Monday		
26	Mars	Tuesday		
27	Mercury	Wednesday		
28	Jupiter	Thursday		Mars Ultori - Ex Gent. Brut.
29	Venus	Friday		
30	Saturn	Saturday		
31	Sun	Sunday	Winter time	

2021 November

Day	Deity	Weekday	Solar Calendar	Lunar Calendar
1	Moon	Monday	Kalendae	
2	Mars	Tuesday		
3	Mercury	Wednesday		
4	Jupiter	Thursday	Ludus Troiae	New Moon 22:!5
5	Venus	Friday	Nonae	Kalendae
6	Saturn	Saturday		Dies Religiosus
7	Sun	Sunday		
8	Moon	Monday	Mundus Patet	Mundus Patet
9	Mars	Tuesday		
10	Mercury	Wednesday		
11	Jupiter	Thursday		First Quarter 13:!8
12	Venus	Friday		Nonae
13	Saturn	Saturday	Idvs Feronia Apollo Soranus	Dies Religiosus
14	Sun	Sunday		
15	Moon	Monday		
16	Mars	Tuesday	Mani familiari	
17	Mercury	Wednesday	Natali Vespasiani	
18	Jupiter	Thursday		
19	Venus	Friday		Idvs (Full Moon 10:00) Fer. - Apollo Sor. Pietas

Appendix 2: Pietas Calendar | 181

2021 November

Day	Deity	Weekday	Solar Calendar	Lunar Calendar
20	Saturn	Saturday		Dies Religiosus
21	Sun	Sunday		
22	Moon	Monday		
23	Mars	Tuesday		
24	Mercury	Wednesday		
25	Jupiter	Thursday		
26	Venus	Friday		
27	Saturn	Saturday		
28	Sun	Sunday		
29	Moon	Monday		
30	Mars	Tuesday		

2021 December

Day	Deity	Weekday	Solar Calendar	Lunar Calendar
1	Mercury	Wednesday	Kalendae ivn-ven-amr-ff-prnptns et pietas	
2	Jupiter	Thursday		
3	Venus	Friday		
4	Saturn	Saturday		Kalendae (New Moon 08:45)Ivn-ven-amr-ff-pr pietas et neptunus
5	Sun	Sunday	Nonae	Dies Religiosus
6	Moon	Monday		
7	Mars	Tuesday		
8	Mercury	Wednesday	Tiber Pater	Tiber Pater
9	Jupiter	Thursday		
10	Venus	Friday	Commemoration Gianfranco Barbera	
11	Saturn	Saturday	Agonium Septimontium	Nonae (First Quarter 02:38) Sol Indiges
12	Sun	Sunday	Dies Natalis Gianfranco Barbera	Dies Religiosus
13	Moon	Monday		

2021 December				
Day	Deity	Weekday	Solar Calendar	Lunar Calendar
14	Mars	Tuesday		
15	Mercury	Wednesday	Consualia	
16	Jupiter	Thursday		
17	Venus	Friday	Saturnalia	Saturnalia
18	Saturn	Saturday	Saturnalia	Saturnalia
19	Sun	Sunday	Saturnalia Opalia	Idvs (Full Moon 05:38) Saturnalia
20	Moon	Monday	Saturnalia	Saturnalia
21	Mars	Tuesday	Saturnalia Divalia 16:56 - Sun in Capricorn	Saturnalia Divalia
22	Mercury	Wednesday	Saturnalia	Saturnalia
23	Jupiter	Thursday	Saturnalia Laurentalia	
24	Venus	Friday	Dies Silenti	
25	Saturn	Saturday	Natalis Solis Invicti	Dies Natalis Solis Invicti
26	Sun	Sunday		
27	Moon	Monday		
28	Mars	Tuesday		
29	Mercury	Wednesday		
30	Jupiter	Thursday	Natalis Divi Titi	
31	Venus	Friday		

Appendix 3: Selected Roman Deities

There are several divinities because the tradition sees the divine in all aspects of the universe. A few important ones that are discussed in the book are presented in this list below.

Aesculapius:

God of medicine. 460 years after the foundation of Rome (293 B.C.E.), an epidemic broke out in Rome. Some Roman sacerdotes were sent to the temple of Asklepios in Epidaurus, in Greece, to seek solutions. There they received a snake belonging to the temple and they were advised to take the snake and set it free in Rome. Upon returning from their trip to Greece, the sacerdotes freed the snake and it went to live on Tiber Island, at the centre of the Tiber river. Here, as suggested by the Greek sacerdotes, a temple was erected in honor of Aesculapius. After the passage to Christianity the temple was converted into a christian hospital, which is active even today. In ancient times many people were healed in this temple. They came for pilgrimage from all over the mediterranean. The archeological excavations here have brought to light numerous votive gifts from such patients. The stories of their miraculous healings are engraved on those items.

Apollo:

Apollo is the God of music, of the different arts his 9 Muse represent, who also stand for the 9 ritual ways within the solar practice, 9 phases of mysteries to whom only the most spiritually evolved people could enter. Apollo is also God of healing practices and is called Savior, for he saves men from illness and is the father of Aesculapius. He is a solar Numen and the acting force that is generated from the power of the Sun, a principle that destroys all its enemies and purifies everything. Apollo is the son of Jupiter and Latona and is the brother of Diana.

Bacchus:

He is one of the sons of Jupiter. His mother is Semele, who died when he still was in her womb. Jupiter took him away from her womb and sewed him onto his thigh , in order to end the gestation/pregnancy. He is the nocturnal counterpart of Apollo. His mysteric rituals were very complex, they were fundamentally based on the "baccano" made during the night, outside the doors of the city. In the bacchan rites, one performed unbridled chants and dances, sometimes accompanied by amorous freedom. Some forms of the dyonisian cult lead into magical orgies, always in the night. Wine is sacred to him, a beverage that helps loosing the inhibitions leading to the euphory of the inebriation when taken in excess. The fundamental distinction between Dyonisus and Apollo lays in the ways in which one makes things. Through Dyonisus one reaches the excess and releases all fears, insticts and concerns. Through Apollo balances are reestablished, which are useful to reach the maturity of the spiritual development.

Castor&Pollux:

In the myth they were known also with the name of Dioscuri, that is sons of Jupiter. They are sons of the Optimus God and Leda, Queen of Sparta. When Jupiter coveted with Leda, having taken the shape of a swan, she laid two eggs: one contained Castor and Clitemnestra, the other Pollux and Helene. When they became deities they ascended to the sky forming the constellation of Gemini. In life Castor was a great horse tamer, while Pollux was a great boxer. During some wars, they were evoked from the Roman Legionnaires, who saw them intervene during the battle dressed as noble knights. When the army returned to Rome, they were seen bringing the horses to water in the Spring of Juturna, to then disappear into nothing. Exactly in that place a temple was erected in their honor.

Ceres:

This deity is related to the crops, cereals are particulary sacred to her. She is the mother of Persephone, the Goddes who gets raped by Hades and brought to the infernal reign, where she becomes Queen of the Underworld. To Ceres and Persephone many mysteries were dedicated in the ancient times, in particular the Eleusinian mysteries in Greece were sacred to them. The emperor Augustus went to Eleusis to be initiated into this ancient wisdom.

Consu:

Deity of the barns, connected to the harvest of the cereals. He had an underground altar at the Circus Maximus. When the Romans raped the Sabines, under the supervision of Romulus, they were inaugurating the altar to the God Consu.

Dia:

Goddess inherent the mysteries reserved to the matrons. Only women could participate to mysteric celebrations made in her honor. Despite this also male sacerdotes had the duty to perform specific cultual acts in the name of the Roman folk. Among these we had the Arval sacerdotes.

Diana:

Diana is the sister of Apollo and his lunar/feminine counterpart. She is the Goddess of hunters, archers, protector of wild animals, children and defenseless beings. Chaste women are vowed to her. She is the protector of virgins and for this reason she represents the purified soul.

Eros/Amor:

Virgil defines Amor as the strongest deity, capable of winning over everything. In the Greek myth Amor is called with the name of Eros, but also has other two specific forms: the abstract love, called Agape and friendship called Filia. Eros, Agape and Filia are three aspects of one identical God: Amor. In the origins of cosmos the God Amor can be found within chaos but in a certain moment acts creating heat thus turning chaos into an ordered world. He is represented with wings because love tends to always run away, in addition to this he is armed with arch and arrows because he suddenly hits people's hearts.

Faunus:

He is the God of forests, flocks, shepherds, of the sylvan aspects of life. He is a chaotic God and was considered by Ovidius the first king of Italy. He is considered the father of Latino, king of the Latins. At the same time he is a God who transmits oracles and makes the purification of the cities possible. In fact during the festivities held in his honor in February, called Lupercalia, Faunus' chaos is freed in the city and purifies it from negativities. The modern Carnival has replaced the ancient festivals of Lupercalia.

Flora:

She is the deity of prosperity. Flowers are sacred to her and between March and the first days of May majestic celebrations were dedicated to her. She is considered to be related to the secret name of the Urbe and to the arcane strenght of the city of Romulus.

Fortuna:

Fortuna is the Goddess of fortune. In the Latium myth, Fortuna is the deity of origins. She is Jupiter and Iuno's mother. To her an enormous sanctuary was erected in the city of Praeneste. Fortuna is composed by two elements: fate and destiny. Fate is the product of our actions, fulfilled in this life; destiny is the product of our ancestors' actions and of our past lives that fall on the individual in this life. She is a very importan mystery deity. Many deities are venerated to improve one's personal relation with Her.

Gaia:

She is the earth Goddess. She is the active and living intelligence of the world, who moves the nature of the living world that surrounds us. In the greek myth Gaia was born directly from chaos and generated from herself the God Uranus, she married him and gave birth to Saturn and other deities. Since Uranus ate his sons, to avoid being dethroned, Gaia built a sickle and gave it to Saturn to emasculate the father taking his place.

Hades:

Greek name of the latin God Dite. He is the King of the Underworld. The Romans feared saying his name, for they could evoke death. For this reason he was called by using appellations; one of the most used was Pluto, that means "the rich" and also "he who gives wealth". The myth tells that Hades, together with his brothers Jupiter and Neptunus fought against his father Saturnus. His weapon was an helmet that made him invisible. In the Eleusinian mysteries the initiations were performed in a temple dedicated to him: the Plutoneyon. This was because the initiates in Eleusis learnt how to die in life and to come back to their bodies right after retaking life.

Hecate:

Hecate is the Goddess that represents the hidden aspect of the Moon.

Hercules:

He is a hero and son of Jupiter. He is the symbol of the initiate, who must face the twelve labours in order to ascend to the Olympus and become a deity. In the myth he is persecuted by Juno; he symbolizes the spirit of the initiate afflicted by soul's passions, of which Juno is sovereign, passions that can be won only by overcoming the twelve labours of Hercules.

Ianus:

Ianus or Janus is a primordial God, he is the chaos of the origins, who contains already within himself the ordering principle. Every start is sacred to him. To Ianus are consecrated the doors because they are passagges, and Ianus presides over every passage, be it of space or time. He is two-faced: wih one he looks back and with the other forwards. When it's war time the doors of Ianus' temple are opened in order to bring the order of peace from the disorder of war.

Isis:

She is an Egyptian winged deity. Isis is the Egyptian counterpart of Juno, since she is also the soul' sovereign. Her wings were always painted in red and blue, because the soul is connected to the body through the blood flow, which is blue if we look at veins and red when it comes to the arteries. She is the wife of Osiris and must face together with her son Thot, the God Seth, who is an evil God of matter who tries to dethronize Osiris. In the myth Seth dismembers Osiris and throws him in the water of Nile. Isis finds the pieces and composes him again, so together with Thot they can win over Seth. Isis is the soul, Thot is the intellect and Osiris the spirit. These three elements oppose the dissolution that comes from the matter.

Juno:

Juno or Iuno is the Goddess of marriage, of fertility, of the domus, of the conjugal love. She is the wife and sister of Jupiter and the mother of Mars, Eris and Vulcanus. She represents loyalty towards the partner. She is the Goddess Queen of the Moon, in fact the first quarter of the Moon is sacred to her, just like the full moon is dedicated to Jupiter.

Jupiter:

Known as Iupiter (Iovis Pater), Jupiter or Iovis, he is the son of Saturn and Opi and the protector of Rome, Iuppiter Optimus Maximus, he who is the greatest. Ius Pater is the father of Law literally, Jupiter is all those metaphysical and physical laws that hold the universe. He is the God of celestial phenomena, of rain, of thunder (Jupiter Tonans), of lightning bolt (Jupiter Fulgur). He is a lightbringer as Jupiter Lucetius, and every month the Ides are dedicated to him – the period of the full moon. The omens that derived from the flight of birds or signs in the sky were referred to Jupiter, and he was venerated throughout Italy on top of the hills and mountains. Jupiter is in everything and everything is in Jupiter, which makes him pantheistic, the ruler of all things.

Limentinus:

From the latin term *Limes*, that is, boundary, he is a deity that presides over boundaries between the human world and the superhuman worlds.

Mania:

Deity of the world of the dead. She is the mother of the Manes, entities that develop based on the actions that men do in life. She was also considered a deity connected to sacred madness, that is to that that allowed people to have mediumistic activities.

Mars:

Mars is the God of Romans, father of Romulus. He is a deity of the cultivated field with strength and energy; at the same time he is the God of defensive war of the fields. He is the energy incarnated in the virile Roman Man, which is farmer and warrior. He makes develop the feel of duty in the man towards his ideals, his nation, his wife, his rituals. Together with Venus he generates his son, the God Amor.

Mercury:

Mercury is the God of dialectic, of silence, of gymnasium, of the intellect, he is gives messages from the Gods and has a psychopompous figure for he can travel between the words. He represents intuition. Mercury is the son of Jupiter and Maya. Mercury is also Lara's husband, who is a nymph. Both are deities of Silence and mystery secrets. From them the Lares are generated, deities who live in the households to protect the families.

Minerva:

Minerva is the Goddess of the mens, of intelligence, artisanship, inventions, of the righteous war and of university. She is the daughter of Jupiter and Metis. Chaste intelligent women are vowed to her. She was born from Jupiter's head, after that Jupiter ate his wife Metis. For this reason in some hymns Jupiter is defined as both father and mother.

Mithra:

He is a solar deity of oriental origin. His cult arrived in Rome in 66 B.C.E. With the Legionnaires of Pompeus, who learnt the cult during the military campaign in Cilicia against the pirates. This ancient God was syncretized with the Sol Invictus and gained great fortune in Rome. In the late antiquity the two greatest religions of the empire were Mithraism and Christianity. The latter persecuted the first until it disappeared. Mithra was born in a cave from a virgin and has 12 disciples. Pagans often accused christians of having created their cult being inspired from the previous one of Mithra.

Moon:

Moon is sister and partner of the Sun. Since the Moon has multiple faces, sometimes she is the virgin Diana, some other time she is Iuno, sister and wife of Jupiter; other times she is the deity Luna when its mystery aspect is called Hecate. She is the deity of the ancient times, in fact the first calendars were lunar ones. The Moon is strictly connected to the feminine nature, in fact his cicle, which is that of the woman, lasts ca. 28 days and a half.

Nemesis:

She is the invisible force that intervene to bring order to the imbalances committed by men. To each unjust and incorrect act Nemesis is unleashed. The worse the act, the greater the quantity of people involved in the revenge of Nemesis, who creates even more disorders to dissolve the imbalances created and bring back the cosmic order.

Neptunus:

He is the God of the seas, of waters and of the occult wisdom. He also symbolize passions, which from the ancients were considered related to the water element. The Cylops are his sons, who are giants with just one eye that symbolize the man victim of his own istincts, with a monocular vision. From the Agathodemonic form of Neptunus, that is in his sublime form, Atlas was born, the mythical king of Atlantis, connoisseur of all the wisdom. He defends the sailors and preserves the mysteric wisdom.

Nilus:

Considered the biggest river of the ancient world, Nilus was believed to be an important God, not only because he gave life to the Egyptian civilization, but also because it brought wisdom to the entire humanity. On the island of Philea, on the Nile river, a centre with many temples was born, from which hermetism arose: the doctrine of the God Hermes (Mercury) who taught the mysteries of the man and of his spiritual realization.

Ops:

Goddess of the pantry, she accompanies the God Saturn, descended to the Latium to bring the teachings of the mysteries to the Latin folk thus initiating the Golden Age. Saturn is connected to the agricoltural production (resulting from the mysteries taught from him) and Ops is connected to the conservation of the food produced.

Osiris:

He is the occult and magical aspect of the Sun in the Egyptian tradition. He is Isis's husband.

Pan:

He like Faunus is a God of forests, flocks, fertility and fields. Pan is every living being that permeates every thing, the almighty deities like Jupiter and Apollo are very often called Pan. Pythagoras said: ***en to pan*** (one in everything) which means that the cosmic deity is in everywhere; Romans said: ***omnia plena Iovis***, inscription that stands out on the modern temple built in honor of Jupiter in Rome, which means everything is full of Jupiter

Picumnus:

He is a Martial deity that comes from the God Picus, the Woodpecker God represented by the axe of war. Picumnus together with Pilumnus drives the negativities away while defending the newborns and the pregnant women.

Pila:

She is the partner of the God Pilum, a deity related to the God Pilumnus. Her function is that to awake his partner, who is a martial deity that defend men from the negativities and has as symbol the spear (***pilum*** in latin).

Pilumnus:

He is a martial deity that is accompanied by the God Pilum, and is also represented by a spear.

Rhea:

Daughter of Uranus and Gaia, sister and wife of Chrono in the skies (Saturn). Her sons were devoured from her husband, who feared to be dethronized from the heavenly throne by them. Rhea hid Jupiter, she fed Saturn with a stone wrapped in the bands of the child. In the meantime Jupiter grew up and having reached the adulthood he freed his brothers from his Father's womb and drove him away from the heavens.

Salus:

She is the Roman Goddess of health. Sometimes she is represented as the wife of Aesculapius, she is accompanied by him, to bring healing. She was evoked by the Roman state in cases of pestilence, with the appellative of Salus Publica. The literal ancient sources mention different occasions in which Salus and Aesculapius saved the Roman folk from terrible pestilences. Salus is also Goddes of hygiene, an element considered to be appropriate to gain good health and to the prevention from the illness' spread.

Saturnus:

Saturn is son of Uranus and Gea and has Rhea as wife. With Her he has as sons and daughters most of the principal Gods: Jupiter, Ceres, Juno, Neptunus, Pluto and Vesta. Agriculture is sacred to him, as well as time (Chrono) and matter (intended as the material world). Saturn is matter and therefore is the God of time because time is the measure of the movement of matter itself. When he evirates his father Uranus Venus is born. This myth means that when in the sky matter was formed, after the Big Bang, the attraction force (Venus) imposed herself in the universe as a fundamental law. As a God of matters, Saturn is also a earthly God, at the same time he is God of the seventh sky, when he gets dethronized by Jupiter he becomes God of the mysteries, who lets men reach the golden era. In the temple of Saturn the ancient Roman held the treasure of the state.

Sol:

While Apollo is the Numen of the Sun, Sol is the Genius of the Sun. The Numen is an acting entity, the Genius is the thinking counterpart. Since the Sun was conceived as a living and thinking being, his name matched with his Genius. The Sun is the celestial body that generates life on earth and takes care of the human kind.

Stercutus:

He is God of purification. He is particulary connected to the purification of the doors of the city and of households. When a woman gives birth, people used to evoke Picumnus and Pilumnus to beat the negativity that came from the faunic world, that is the instictive extraurban world, and Stercutus in order for him to drive these forces away.

Tiber Pater (Tiberinus):

He is the river Tiber, that had many appellatives. This deity was the intelligence sovereign of the river itself, that saved Romulus and Remus and fed the sacred city of Rome. Since the existence of Rome was connected to this God, he received a proper cult and honors in his name.

Uranus:

He is the God of the sky, father of Saturn. Uranus ate his sons not to be dethronized, but his son Saturn was saved and brought up in secret. When he (Saturn) grew up, he faced his father and evirated him with a sickle, which is also his symbol. From the sperm of Uranus, that fell onto the sea, Venus was born.

Vediovis:

Archaic Roman deity, connected to a juvenile and mysteric aspect of Jupiter. He is connected to the solar aspect of the young Jupiter, in fact he was represented with arch and arrows like Apollo.

Venus:

Venus is the Goddess of attraction, love, sexuality, fertility, flowers, gardens, spring as Venus Felix, Victrix and Genetrix but she is also she who inspires the ideas of men as Venus Ourania or Pandemos. She is also Enea's mother, founder of the Roman civilization, making her mother of the Romans. She was born during spring from the foam of the sea fertilized by the genitals of Uranus that Saturn had thrown into the sea after the rebellion against his father.

Vulcanus:

God of fire and God of blacksmith. The weapons that he builds are invincible and magic. He fabricated the weapons of the hero Achilles, Hades' helmet, the shield of Aeneas, the arch and the arrows of Apollo and Diana, Mercury's helmet and sandals, the shield of Jupiter, Cupid's arch and arrows (the greek Eros). Vulcanus is the first husband of Venus, he represents the necessary fire to forge the spiritual weapons of the initiates and of the heroes.

Appendix 4: Of the Wonderful Natures of Fire and Earth

There are two things, saith Hermes, viz., Fire and Earth, which are sufficient for the operation of all wonderful things: the former is active, the latter passive. Fire, as saith Dionysius, in all things, and through all things, comes and goes away bright; it is in all things bright, and at the same time occult and unknown. When it is by itself (no other matter coming to it, in which it should manifest its proper action) it is boundless and invisible, of itself sufficient for every action that is proper to it, movable, yielding itself after a manner to all things that come next to it, renewing, guarding Nature, enlightening, not comprehended by lights that are veiled over, clear, parted, leaping back, bending upwards, quick in motion, high, always raising motions, comprehending another, not comprehended itself, not standing in need of another, secretly increasing of itself, and manifesting its greatness to things that receive it; Active, Powerful, Invisibly present in all things at once; it will not be affronted or opposed, but as it were in a way of revenge, it will reduce, on a sudden, things into obedience to itself; incomprehensible, impalpable, not lessened, most rich in all dispensations of itself. Fire, as saith Pliny, is the boundless and mischievous part of the nature of things, it being a question whether it destroys or produceth most things. Fire itself is one, and penetrates through all things, as say the Pythagoreans, also spread abroad in the Heavens, and shining: but in the infernal place straitened, dark and tormenting; in the mid way it partakes of both. Fire, therefore, in itself is one, but in that which receives it, manifold; and in differing subjects it is distributed in a different manner, as Cleanthes witnesseth in Cicero. That fire, then, which we use is fetched out of other things. It is in stones, and is fetched out by the stroke of the steel; it is in Earth, and makes that, after digging up, to smoke; it is in Water, and heats springs and wells; it is in the depth of the Sea, and makes that, being tossed with winds, warm; it is in the Air, and makes it (as we oftentimes see) to burn. and all animals and living things whatsoever, as also all vegetables, are preserved by heat; and every thing that lives, lives by reason of the inclosed heat. The properties of the Fire that is above, are heat, making all things fruitful, and light, giving life to all things. The properties of the infernal Fire are a parching heat, consuming all things, and darkness, making all things barren. The Celestial and bright Fire drives away spirits of darkness; also this, our Fire made with wood, drives away the same in as much as it hath an analogy with and is the vehiculum of that Superior light; as also of him who saith, " I am the Light of the World," which is true Fire, the Father of Lights, from whom every good thing, that is given, comes; sending forth the light of His Fire, and communicating it first to the Sun and the rest of the Celestial bodies, and by these, as by mediating instruments, conveying that light into our Fire. As, therefore, the spirits of darkness are stronger in the dark, so good spirits, which are Angels of Light, are augmented, not only by that light, which is Divine, of the Sun, and Celestial, but also by the light of our common Fire. Hence it was that the first and most wise institutors of religions and ceremonies ordained that prayers, singings and all manner of divine worships whatsoever should not be performed without lighted candles or torches (hence, also, was that significant saying of Pythagoras, "Do not speak of God without a Light"), and they commanded that for the driving away of wicked spirits, Lights and Fires should be kindled by the corpses of the dead, and that they should not be removed until the expiations were after a holy manner performed and they buried. And the great

Jehovah himself in the old law commanded that all his sacrifices should be offered with Fire, and that Fire should always be burning upon the altar, which custom the priests of the altar did always observe and keep amongst the Romans.

Now the basis and foundation of all the Elements the Earth, for that is the object, subject, and receptacle of all Celestial rays and influences; in it are contained the seeds and seminal virtues of all things; and therefore it is said to be Animal, Vegetable and Mineral. It being made fruitful by the other Elements and the Heavens, it brings forth all things of itself. It receives the abundance of all things and is, as it were, the first fountain from whence all things spring. It is the center, foundation and mother of all things. Take as much of it as you please, separated, washed, depurated, subtilized, if you let it lie in the open air a little while, it will, being full and abounding with heavenly virtues, of itself bring forth plants, worms and other living things, also stones, and bright sparks of metals. In it are great secrets, if at any time it shall be purified by the help of Fire, and reduced unto its simplicity by a convenient washing. It is the first matter of our creation, and the truest medicine that can restore and preserve us.

Chapter V, Of the wonderful natures of fire and earth, The Philosophy of Natural Magic.

By Henry Cornelius Agrippa Von Nettesheim.,

Published by The de Laurence Company, Chicago IL, 1913. This book is in the Public Domain and there are no known copyright restrictions in the United States on the use of the text.

Glossary

Accipitridae: one of the three families within the order Accipitriformes, are a family of small to large birds with strongly hooked bills and variable morphology based on diet.

Ager: Field

Amphiteatrum Flavium: Flavian Amphitheatre

Annales Pontificum: Pontiff's annals

Argiletum: Was the main route approaching the Forum Romanum from the northeast in the ancient city of Rome.

Auctoritas: Authority

Augur: Diviner

Auguraculum: Roofless temple oriented to the cardinal points, in which the priests of ancient Rome practiced augury and ornithomancy.

Ausculum: Ausculum Picenum, the modern day Ascoli Piceno, an Italian city situated in the Marche region.

Bacchanalia: Bacchanalia

Basilica Aemilia: It was a civil Basilica in the Roman forum

Collis Capitolinus: Capitol

Captio: Capture, custody.

Cardo: Pole, axis, chief point

Cives: The citizens

Cives Romanus: Roman citizens

Civis Romanus sum: I am a Roman citizen

Clavifixio: The act of putting a nail on the wall

Clavus Annalis: Chronicles of this specific rite. Clavus literally means Nail.

Clusius: An epiteth of Janus, because in time of piece his temple remained close.

Coelo: Sky

Collis Capitolinus: Capitoline hill

Commentarii Pontificum: Pontifex's comments

Compitum: Intersection

Daemon or Daimon(Greek): Tutelary Deity

Decamanus: The streets that ran east-west

Decemvirs: Ten men

Dionysiae: The Dionysiae were festivals dedicated to Dionysus. It was particularly popular in Athens. During the festival there was first a series of public rituals followed by a procession in which sacred symbols such as terracotta vines, herms and wine kraters were displayed. Then a series of competitive cultural activities of theatrical nature took place. These included choruses, comedies and tragedies, where themes related to the myth of the God were performed.

Fetiales: A fetial was a type of priest in ancient Rome. They formed a collegium devoted to Jupiter as the patron of good faith.

Filius Martis: Son of Mars

Flamen: Priest of specific deity A flamen was a priest of the ancient Roman religion who was assigned to one of eighteen deities with official cults during the Roman Republic.

Forma mentis: Mindset

Forum Romanum: The city hall

Fratres Arväles: Arval brothers were a body of priests who offered annual sacrifices to the Lares and Gods to guarantee good harvests. Inscriptions provide evidence of their oaths, rituals and sacrifices.

Genius Loci: Tutelary God of an area

Genius: Guardian Angel or Spiritual Guide

Gloria: Glory

Haruspex: Diviner

Hastae Martiae: Spear of God Mars

Homines: Men

Homo: Man

Honor: Honor

Humus: Mud

Ignis: Fire

Imperium Domi: The power of the consul within the city of Rome

Imperium Maius: The power of the consul in the world outside the boundaries of the city of Rome

Imperium: Empire

Infere: below, underneath, lower,

Infero: Inherent to what I carry (fero) inside(in), bear in

Insignia: A distinguishing badge or emblem of military rank, office, or membership of an organization.

Insigno: Engrave

Intercessio Tribunicia: The power of veto of the tribune of the plebs against the acts of the magistrates

Iovis Optimi maximi capitolini: Temple of Jupiter Optimus Maximus on the Capitoline hill.

Iugum: The collar with which the oxen were tied to pull the plow. When it's intended in its symbolism relating to the doors, it refers to the man going out to work (like a tied ox) and returning home (being freed) removing the yoke.

Iure Pater Familia: Rightful father of the family, that is, the head of the household.

Ius: Law

Janiculum: Hill in western Rome

Kalendae: New Moon

Lapis niger: Literally black stone, it is an ancient shrine in the Roman Forum.

Lararium: the shrine of the Lares in an ancient roman home Cives Romanus: Roman citizen

Lares compitales: household deities of the crossroads

Lari:tutelary God/Gods of home/hearth/crossroads

Lex Vetusta: Ancient law

Libri Sacerdotum Populi Romani Quiritium: Books of the priests of the Roman people

Lituo: Curved augural staff

Lituus: Prayer

Logos: Word, reason

Magister populi: Military collaborator of the rex during the period of the royal age of Rome and appointed by him

Magistrates: Magistrates

Mens: Mind/Spirit

Nihil difficile amanti puto: nothing is difficult for the person who loves.

Nonae: First quarter Moon

Ides: Full Moon

Numen: Deity/Divine will

Omen: Sign, token

Omnia vincit Amor et nos cedamus amori: Love conquers all things; let us yield to love.

Pacis deum exposcendae causa: Because it was necessary to insist on the peace with the Gods

Pagus, pagi: Village, villages

Pater patriae: Fatherland's father

Patulcius: an epiteth of Janus, because in time of war his temple stood open

Pax Deorum: Peace between men and the Gods

Penates: Household Gods worshipped in conjunction with Vesta and the Lares. The Penates are the deities worshipped by the family and are represented in the Lararium, the small temple in Roman houses in front of which rituals were performed. In ancient Mesopotamia, the Assyrians already emulated the act of constant prayer before the God by placing their own statuettes in the act of prayer in front of the Gods. Placing one's own image in front of that of the Gods corresponds to being always present to do their duty towards the Gods and to being under their guidance and protection.

Pietas: Piety, devotion, sense of duty, and loyalty to Gods, country and friends and family.

Pomerium: Space left free from buildings round walls of Roman/Etruscan town (esp. Rome)

Pontifex: High priest. The plural Pontifices.

Praetor Maximus: One who has the highest office in the Republic. Praetor is someone who has a public office. The law said Praetor Maximum because at any time the highest office could be different. For example, the King was the highest praetor. In the Republic he is the oldest consul, but if a dictator is elected, he is the praetor.

Primus Potitius: The pater familias of the Potizii family

Princeps Civitatis: Prince of the city

Provocatio Ad Populum: an institution of Roman public law, introduced by the Lex Valeria de provocatione of 509 BC. (signed by the consul Publius Valerius Publicola) and applied in particular in the Republican period.

Quindecemviri sacris faciundi: the fifteen members of a college with priestly duties.

Ratio: Reason

Religio: Religion, superstition, worship

Rex Sacrorum: King of sacred things

Rex: King

Rituarium: Set of rituals Vati: Bards

Salutatio: Formal greeting

Saturnia tellus: Saturn's land. It indicates the reign of the God Saturn during the mythical Golden Age, which he initiated, after his expulsion from Olympus.

Septemviri epulonum: The seven men assigned to the sacred banquets

Septimontium: Seven hills

Serapeum: A serapeum is a temple or other religious institution dedicated to the syncretic Greco - Egyptian deity Serapis, who combined aspects of Osiris and Apis in a humanized form that was accepted by the Ptolemaic Greek of Alexandria

Sive Supertitio: Or superstition

Sodales Titii: Was a college (sodalitas) of Roman priests.

Somnium Scipionis: Scipio's dream

Supere: Superior, above

Thus: Incense

Urbe: City. The city of Rome is often referred to as Urbe as a homage to the ancient sacred city.

Vaticini: Predictions

Velabro: It was the name of the valley that stretched between the northeastern slopes of the Palatine and Capitoline Hill.

Veritas: Truth

Via Sacra: Sacred street

Vigilantes: Guardians

Vir: Man, related to the world virtue, opposed to homo which is "made of humus".

Virgo: Virgin

Viri clarissimi: Plural form of vir clarissimus, the definition of any member of the senatorial order. It means illustrious men.

Vis: Strength

Bibliography

Agrippa von Nettesheim, Heinrich Cornelius, Reghini, Arturo, and Alberto, Fidi. La Filosofia Occulta o la Magia. Rome: Edizioni Mediterranee, 1972.

Alessandro, Roccati, and Carmela, Maria B. Eggitologia. Rome: Libreria dello Stato , 2005.

Alföldy, Géza. Storia sociale dell'antica Roma. Bologna: Il Mulino, 1987.

Barbera, Giuseppe. Pitagorismo in Italia ieri e oggi. Rome: Streetlib, 2005.

Bartoloni, Gilda. Le società dell'Italia primitiva. Rome: Carocci, 1992.

Bianchi, Bandinelli. La fine dell'arte antica. Milan: BUR Biblioteca Universiti Rizzoli , 2000.

Bickerman, E J. La cronologia nel mondo antico. Firenze: La Nuova Italia, 1963.

Carandini, Andrea. La nascita di Roma : dèi, Lari, eroi e uomini all'alba di una civiltà. Torino: Einaudi, 1997.

Corpus Inscriptionum Latinarum. Berlin: Berlin-Brandenburg Academy of Sciences and Humanities, 1871-2003.

D'Anna, Gabriella. Dizionario dei miti. Rome: Tascabili Economici Newton, 1996.

Garnsey, Saller. Storia economica e sociale dell'impero romano. Londra: , 1987.

Giardina, Andrea. L'uomo Romano. Bari: Laterza, 1990.

Gruppo di Ur, . Introduzione alla Magia. Rome: Edizioni Mediterranee, 1971.

Kremmerz, Giuliano. La scienza dei Magi. Rome: Edizioni Mediterranee, 1974-1975.

Limentani, Ida C. Epigrafia Latina. Milan: Istituto Editoriale Universitario, 1991.

Montanari, Enrico. Mito e storia nell' annalistica romana delle origini. Rome: Ateneo, 1990.

Montanari, Enrico. Momenti di una presa di coscienza culturale. Rome: Bulzoni, 1976.

Pallottino, Massimo. Etruscologia. Milan: Hoepli, 1984.

Rosati, Giuseppe. Via Latina, Antologia di autori latini. Milan: Sansoni, 1996.

Rutilio, Claudio. Pax Deorum. Italy: SeaR, 1989.

Notes

1. See glossary, ***Cives Romanus***.

2. See glossary, ***Urbe***.

3. The ban on celebrating Bacchanals was undertaken to stop the dangerous incidents that took place during these orgiastic ceremonies, where there were even cases of self-harm among the participants.

4. See glossary, ***Pietas***.

5. See glossary, ***Gloria***. See glossary, Honor.

6. The Roman tradition has not remained the same since its birth. It has absorbed elements of other traditions too, like that of the Etruscans, to become what we know nowadays as Traditio Romana.

7. See bibliography, Pallottino, Massimo, pp. 322 and following.

8. See bibliography, Carandini, Andrea, pp. 5 and following.

9. Ibidem.

10. See glossary, ***Pagi***.

11. See bibliography, Carandini, Andrea. Very interesting are Andrea Carandini's attempts to try to connect the historical and archaeological data with ancient sources, following the thread of mythological history in his cited book. Massimo Pallottino deals with the problem of the first Italian settlements and of the migrations that took place in the peninsula.

12. See bibliography, Carandini, Andrea.

13. See bibliography, Carandini, Andrea, pp. 5 and following.

14. See ancient historical work by Titius Livius, Ab Urbe Condita, chapter I, paragraph VII.

15. Ibidem.

16. Referring to the God Pan. See Appendix 3, Pan.

17. See glossary, ***Via Sacra***.

18. Janus manifests himself not only in the physical world, but also in our spiritual path through the initiation ritual. We are initiated into the spiritual life on the day we wear the ***toga***. From that day we start struggling against our own selves and against our internal demons. We need to be purified to reach our fullfilment. Even simple gentiles can reach the apotheosis of the emperors by the power of this purity. In this way the janual nature

manifests within us.

19. See ancient historical work by Titius Livius, Ab Urbe Condita, I.19.2. See Carandini, Andrea pp. 296, note n. 57.

20. See bibliography, Carandini, Andrea, p. 295.

21. See bibliography, Carandini, Andrea. According to Carandini the army passing through the eastern entrance is as if it is passing below a triumphal arch.

22. See glossary, **lapis niger**.

23. Not to be confused with the homonymous Egyptian God Khonsu belonging to the theology of the New Kingdom.

24. It is fair to say that the Roman man is free because the ritual passage from boyhood to manhood in the Roman patriciate takes place with an initiation that occurs on March 17, a day sacred to the God Libero, a particular aspect of the God Jupiter.

25. See bibliography, Carandini, Andrea, p. 162.

26. The ancient demon has nothing to do with the Christian concept of it. Socrates explains that the Greek demons (corresponding to what the Romans called Genius) can be good or bad and each, according to his **Pietas**, can embody a cacodaemon or an agathodaemon.

27. See bibliography, Carandini, Andrea, p. 162.

28. In the Roman funeral epigraphs, the deceased dear to us are entrusted to the Gods Mani.

29. See bibliography, Carandini, Andrea, pp. 160-161.

30. A characteristic proper of the Roman tradition is to see in the practitioners who perform a ritual the incarnation of deities, who, through the tools attributed to each Gods, execute the rite.

31. See bibliography, Carandini, Andrea, Carandini, p. 511.

32. See bibliography, Bartoloni, Gilda.

33. See ancient historical work by Titius Livius, Ab Urbe Condita, Chapter I and XX.

34. Pompey's son offered an ecatomb of bulls to Neptune in the hope of gaining favour in the naumachiae against Octavian Augustus. He performed the rite when it was not prescribed and forced certain energies, thus creating an imbalance. His unsanctioned and superstitious act therefore couldn't win over the power of Augustus's **Pietas**, which helped Augustus win over Pompey's son in the struggle for power in Rome.

35. The God Janus could be well compared to St. Peter, holder of the keys of paradise. It can be compared to the guardian of the threshold of the Steinerians.

36. Reason for which the temple was defined as the physical dwelling of the deity to which it was dedicated.

37. See ancient historical work by Titius Livius, Ab Urbe Condita, Chapters I and XVIII.

38. See ancient historical work by Vitruvius, De Architectura, Chapter IV.

39. See glossary, Dionysia.

40. Cities of the Roman Empire such as Palmyra, or the numerous centers scattered in the Spanish Meseta, were constantly supplied with water thanks to the imposing hydraulic works that these people were able to build. This is clearly in contrast with what some scholars claim, that is, that the Romans and the Latin people were an underdeveloped society.

41. See bibliography, Alföldy, Géza and bibliography, Garnsey, Saller. The order of the knights in ancient Rome was composed of the rich plebeians, those who in ancient times could afford to get a horse for war. These two books are useful in better understanding ancient Rome's social order.

42. Literally "the fifteen men of the sacred things that must be done".

43. See bibliography, Limentani, Ida p. 379.

44. See bibliography, Marini, L. or biblography, Limentani, Ida to deepen your knowledge about this topic.

45. See bibliography, Montanari, Enrico, Roma, Momenti di una presa di coscienza culturale. This book provides more clarification on the esoteric work carried out by Quintus Fabius Maximus Cuncator (temporeggiatore).

46. The real esoteric calendar is based on both the cycles of the Sun and the Moon. The Maya, who were more precise than the Romans added the cycle of Venus to this calculation and they were able to understand how many years the earth returned to the same position with respect to the Moon, the Sun and the Venus.

47. See bibliography Bickermann, E, pp. 19-20.

48. See historical work by Cicerone, In Verrem 2.2.129 and Ibid. pp. 41.

49. Plural form of pontifex.

50. See bibliography Rutilio, Claudio, p. 48.

51. There are authors who assert that the Vestals were not really virgins, but that they practiced sexual magic with the **Pontifex Maximus**. To support this false thesis they take the meaning of the word virgo as "vir - go" and claim that it actually indicates their non - chastity. Obviously such conjectures are not enough to support such an exaggerated thesis. The priestesses in charge of the highest, most conscious and noble sexual magic were the flaminicae, **Flamines**' wives. The priestesses of Venus performed a different kind of sexual magic and were more easily open to others, whereas the flaminicae could not have

extra-marital relations, since they had to embody forces that were developed in harmony with *eros*, which means love and not sex, as some ungodly people of other religions want us to believe. In conclusion, the importance of the virgin's function is so high that she could not profane the fire to which she was guardian with sexuality becuase if she were to do so it would result in the destruction of Romanity.

52. See bibliography Rutilio, Claudio, p. 55.

53. See bibliography, Montanari, Enrico, Mito e Storia nell'annalistica romana delle origini, p. 85.

54. See glossary, Clavifixo.

55. XVI dies ante Kalendas aprilis, the day on which the Kite, the bird of the birth of consciousness, rises and the day on which the constellation of Pisces begins to set.

56. See Glossary, **Penates**.

57. In this way the the lustration of the statuettes and figurines in the **Lararium**, as well as the lamps or candelabra and the purification of the ritual robes would be carried out.

58. Some attribute the semantic origin of "Hero" to **Eros**, God of love.

59. According to other sources Venus is Uranus' daughter.

60. It would be more correct to say that Jupiter is opposed to the reign of Saturn, fighting it, emasculating him and sending him away from Olympus, finally laying new laws for a new kingdom of the Gods.

61. Twelve are the companions of Jason, as well as twelve are the knights chosen by King Arthur, twelve the apostles of Mithras and twelve those of Christ, twelve are the chosen Gods and twelve are the months of the solar year.

62. So are called the seven rails in myths like the Mesopotamian one of Enlili and Ninlil.

63. Love conquers all things and so we too shall yield to love.

64. See the section, The Mysteries of Saturn in this book.

65. On the hermetic references of the Romans in the practice of agriculture see the writing of Macrobius: The Saturnalia.

66. Bards.

67. Penelope's suitors.

68. Starting from Spring Equinox to thirty days after that date.

Index

Accipitridae, 11, 194

Achilles, 114, 191

Adoniac, 82

Aeneas, xiv, 87, 94, 109, 191

Aeneid, xii, xiv, 80, 95, 109, 111

Aesculapius, 183, 190

Ager, 17, 194

Agrippa, 17, 32, 83,

Alaric, 15

Alba Longa, 9, 10

Alexandria, 62, 129,130, 198

Amaryllis, 13

Amphiteatrum Flavium, 194

Amulius, 9, 10

Ancus Marcius, 38

Androgyny, 101

Andromeda, xiv, 96, 98, 99, 103

Annales Pontificum, 56, 194

Apollo, xiv, 69, 126, 141, 144, 145, 156, 161, 163, 164, 165, 175, 176, 180, 183, 184, 189, 190, 191

Apuleius, 62, 66, 69, 81, 90, 121

Arch of Marcus Aurelius, xiii, 2

Argiletum, 23, 194

Aries, 55, 83, 84, 91, 107, 116, 134, 167, 171, 187, 196

Aristotle, 148, 167

Asylum, 13, 14

Auctoritas, 194

Augur, 184, 194, 197

Auguraculum, 39, 194

Augustus, xiv, 58, 69, 95, 109, 111, 158, 184, 202

Augustus, xiv, 58, 95, 109, 111, 202

Ausculum, 9, 194

Aventine Hill, 10

Babylonians, 55

Bacchanalia, 194

Bacchus, 110, 183

Barbera, xiv, 129, 131, 135, 136, 147, 163, 181, 200,

Basilica Aemilia, 23, 194

Big Bang, 148, 190

Bishop, 129, 130

Bolsena Mirror, 116

Bruno, 81, 131

Byzantine, 62

Calabria, 47, 148, 163

Capricorn, 109, 182

Captio, 56, 194

Carandini, 9, 25, 39, 200, 201, 202

Cardo, 21, 194

Carmenta, 19

Carmentalis, 57

Carmi, 155

Carthaginians, 53, 155

Castor & Pollux, 183, 184

Castores, 41, 44, 192

Cato, 47, 127

Celeus, 110

Celsus, 62, 80

Ceres, 90, 110, 119, 184, 190

Cerialis, 57

Cesarian reform, 54

Chaldean priests, 49

Chaos, 89

Charlemagne

Charybdis, 114

Christianity, 100, 125, 188

Chrysomallos, 107

Cicero, 16, 55, 62, 80, 136, 192

Circe, 114

Cives, 194

Civis Romanus 12, 194

Civis Romanus sum, 12, 194

Claudius, 19, 80

Clavifixio, 194

Clavus Annalis, xi, 58, 194

Clusius, 194

Coelo, 40, 195

Colchis, 107

College of the Fratres Arvales, 52

Collis Capitolinus, 5, 194, 195

Collis Capitolinus, 5, 56, 194, 195

Commentarii Pontificum, 56, 195

Compita, 21

Compitalia, 169

Consu, 184

Consul Caius Flaminius, 53

Creonus, 85

Cronos, 89, 91

Crotone University Consortium, 148

Cyclop, 84, 114, 188

D.Ulansey 98

Daemon or Daimon(Greek), 195

Danae, 98

De Architectura, 42, 148, 203

De Magia, xii, 5, 117, 121

Decamanus, 21, 195

Decemvirs, 53, 195

Dia, 50, 52, 184

Dialis, 57

Diana, 172, 183, 184, 188, 191

Diocletian, 39, 118, 160

Dionysia, 203

Easter, 84

Ebla, 129

Eclogues, 80, 109

Egypt, 82, 84, 120

Egyptian order, 127, 130

Eleusinian, 44, 110, 141, 184, 185

Eleusis, 161

Enlightenment, 3, 35, 107

Erice, 53

Eros/Amor, 13, 90, 103, 104, 148, 184, 191, 204

Esoterism, 44

Ethiopia, 3

Etruscan, 9, 17, 28, 58, 197

Eupaco, 148

Evander, 19

Exoterism, xi, 44

Falacer, 57

Faunus, 20, 27, 185

Fetiales, 50, 195

Filius Martis, 15, 195

Fiumicino, 52

Flamen, 57, 195

Flora, 13, 163, 185

Floralia, 13, 173

Floralis, 57

Fordicidia, 84, 172

Forma mentis, 62, 195

Fortuna, 82, 89, 175, 185

Forum Romanum, 21, 195

France, 3

Fratres Arvales 50, 52

Furrinalis, 57

Gaia, 90, 185, 189

Garbati, 100, 105

Genius Loci, xiii, 36, 37, 79, 195

Genius, 36, 62, 64, 65, 115, 116, 190, 195, 202

Gentile, iv, 38, 65, 71, 76, 116, 119, 125, 129, 130, 134, 136, 149, 163, 165

Georgics, xii, 80, 109, 110

Gloria, 195, 201

Golden Age, 14, 189, 198

Golden Fleece, xii, 107

Great Kite, 83

Greece, xix, 183

Greek-roman mythology, 67

Hades, 98, 185

Hannibal, 54

Haruspex, xi, 47, 195

Hastae Martiae, 28, 195

Hecate, 186, 188

Hercules, 19, 36, 37, 67, 82, 85, 186

Hermetic academies, 127

Hermeticism, 44, 107, 125, 131, 136

Hesiod, 112, 148

Homer, 47, 112

Homeric Hymns, 80

Homines, 195

Homo, 195

Honor, 195, 201

Honorius, 15

Hubris, 104, 115

Humus, 196

Hypatia, 130

Ianus, 186

Ignis, 83, 196

Iliad, 80, 95

Imperium Domi, 39, 196

Imperium maius, 39, 196

Imperium, 196

Incense, 198

Infere, 196

Infero, 196

Initiate, 19, 37, 46, 67, 68, 74, 84, 85, 98, 114, 127, 147

Initiation, xi, 66

Insignia, 196

Intercessio Tribunicia, 58, 196

Iolco, 107

Iovis Optimi maximi capitolini, 21, 196

Isis, 19, 186

Italy, iv, xiii, xiv, xix, xx, 3, 4, 94, 102, 126, 127, 129, 130, 134, 141, 143, 144, 145, 146, 149, 156, 162, 163, 167, 185, 200

Iugum, 25, 196

Iure Pater Familia, 65, 196

Ius, 17, 196

Janiculum, 116, 196

Janus, 14, 23, 35, 36, 36, 186, 194, 197

Jason, 107, 204

Julius, xiv, 15, 83, 96, 109

Juno Lucina, 91

Juno, 19, 31, 87, 90, 186, 190

Jupiter Stator, 43

Jupiter, 11, 12, 14, 17, 19, 28, 31, 50, 57, 83, 90, 91, 103, 149, 154, 166, 169, 170, 171, 172, 173, 174, 175, 176, 177, 178, 179, 180, 181, 182, 183, 184, 186, 187, 188, 189, 190, 191, 202

Kalendae, 166, 167, 169, 170, 171, 172, 174, 175, 177, 178, 179, 180, 196

King Arthur, 107, 204

Kremmerz, xiv, 91, 107, 127, 128, 200

Kroton, xiv, xiv, 137, 138

La Scienza dei Magi, 107, 200

Lapis niger, 22, 23, 90, 120, 196, 202,

Lara, 187

Lararium, 35, 36, 166, 196, 197, 204

Lares Compitales, 21

Lari, 196, 200

Latin language, 64

Latium, 89

Lex Vetusta, 58, 196

Libri Sacerdotum Populi Romani Quiritium, 56, 196

Limentinus, 187

Lituo, 197

Lituus, 197

Livius, 19, 39, 58, 201, 202, 203

Logos, 24, 197

Lunations, 55

Lunisolar calendar, 55

Lupercalia, 50, 170, 185

Luperci, 50

Lydia, 119

Macrobius, 80, 204

Magic, xii, 32, 119, 193

Magister populi, 53, 120, 197

Magistrates, 20, 39, 52, 56, 196, 197

Magliana, 52

Magna Grecia, 69, 127

Magna Mater, 119

Mana, 25

Mars, 10, 11, 23, 25, 28, 31, 37, 50, 57, 83, 155, 166, 169, 170, 171, 172, 173, 174, 175, 176, 177, 178, 179, 180, 181, 182, 187, 195

Marta Sordi, 58

Martialis, 57

Matthiae, 129

Medusa, 98, 98, 100, 103

Megara, 85

Mens, 53, 54, 62, 174, 197

Mercury, 11, 23, 24, 112, 115, 119, 120, 126, 161, 169, 170, 171, 172, 173, 174, 175, 176, 177, 178, 179, 180, 181, 182, 187, 188

Merlin, 107

Mesopotamia, 47, 55

Meton of Athens, 55

Michelangelo, 131

Middle ages, 119, 162

Minerva, 87, 91, 103, 104, 171, 187

Minervae Medicae, 141

Mithra, 69, 115, 188

Monad, 101

Monotheism, 6

Moon, 23, 24, 101, 112, 167, 168, 169, 170, 171, 172, 173, 174, 175, 176, 177, 178, 179, 180, 181, 182, 186, 187, 188, 196, 197, 203

Moses, 115

Mount Olympus, 31

Museum of Etruscology of Villa Giulia in Rome, 49

Myriam, 19

Mysteries, xi, 82

Mythology, 5, 6, 9, 19, 44, 67, 89, 95, 97, 101

Naples, xiv, 94, 129, 130, 130

Napoleon, 3

Narni, 15

Nemesis, 188

Neptune, 104, 114

New York, 99, 100

Nihil difficile amanti puto, 13, 197

Nile, 129, 186, 188

Nilo, 129

Nonae, 78, 168, 169, 170, 171, 172, 173, 174, 177, 179, 180, 181, 197

Numen, 62, 65, 66, 69, 74, 76, 78, 109, 148, 183, 190, 197

Numitor, 9, 10

Odysseus/Ulysses

Olgiata, 141, 164

Olympius, 130

Olympus, 31, 85, 186, 198, 204

Omen, 11, 109, 197

Omnia vincit Amor et nos cedamus amori, 13, 197,

Ops, 28, 29, 189

Index | 215

Orphic hymn, 76, 80, 101

Osiris, 62, 82, 186, 189, 198

Ovid, 89

Pacis deum exposcendae causa, 58, 197

Pagus, 9, 74, 126, 197

Palatine hill, 9, 10, 14, 19, 24, 25, 28, 50, 199

Palatualis, 57

Palermo, xiv, 141, 144, 165

Pan, 42, 189, 201

Panciera, 39

Paris, 112

Pater patriae, 15, 197

Patulcius, 23, 197

Pax Deorum, 53, 56, 58, 197, 200

Pegasus, 98, 103, 104

Pelias, xiv, 106, 107

Penates, 35, 83, 116, 197, 204

Penelope, xiv, 19, 46, 99, 113, 114, 204

Perseus, xii, xiv, 67, 96, 98, 99, 100, 102, 103, 104, 105, 107

Phrygian Cabeirian mysteries, 82

Piacenza, xiii, 48, 127

Pico della Mirandola 131

Picumnus, 25, 27, 189, 190

Pietas, i, iii, xi, xii, 15, 35, 37, 38, 70, 80, 125, 126, 129, 134, 149, 160, 161, 162, 163, 180, 197, 201, 202, 202

Piety, 35, 109, 136, 197

Pila, 25, 189

Pilumnus, 25, 27, 189, 190

Plethon, 131

Plutarch, 12, 14, 62, 80

Polidette, 98

Polyphemus, 84, 114

Polytheism, 6

Pomerium, xi, 11, 17, 19, 20, 23, 39, 158, 197

Pomonalis, 57

Pompilius, 31, 39, 40

Pontifex, 28, 31, 32, 43, 50, 54, 55, 56, 109, 120, 148, 153, 197, 203,

Pope Innocentius, 15

Pordenone, xiv, 141, 143

Portunalis, 57

Potizii, 19, 36, 198

Praetor Maximus, 58, 197

Primus Potitius, 36, 37, 198

Princeps Civitatis, 109, 198

Proci, 20, 114

Provocatio Ad Populum, 58, 198

Psyche, 90

Punic, 14, 53, 81, 154, 155

Pythagoras, 17, 62, 67, 136, 148, 192

Quindecemviri sacris faciundi, 50, 198

Quintus Fabius Maximus 53, 203

Quirinalis, 57

Quirinus, 15, 23, 50, 57

Ratio, 62, 198

Red Sea, 115

Index | 217

Religio, 37, 198

Remus, 9, 10, 11, 20, 32, 57, 190

Rex Sacrorum, 28, 50, 72, 198

Rex, 15, 28, 32, 50, 72, 197, 198

Rhea Silvia, 9, 10, 20, 57

Rhodians, 43

Rituarium, 198

Roman civilization, 3, 12, 149, 191

Rome, xi, xiii, xiv, 2, 3, 4, 9, 10, 12, 13, 15, 16, 17, 19, 21, 23, 24, 26, 28, 31, 35, 39, 40, 43, 49, 50, 54, 55, 56, 57, 58, 59, 70, 74, 82, 85, 85, 109, 110, 119, 121, 134, 134, 141, 146, 152, 153, 154, 159, 160, 163, 164, 165, 183, 184, 187, 188, 189, 190, 194, 195, 196, 197, 200, 202

Romulus, xi, 5, 9, 10, 11, 12, 13, 14, 17, 18, 19, 20, 24, 28, 31, 32, 40, 43, 46, 57, 83, 85, 109, 166, 184, 185, 187, 190

Sabines, 31, 43, 184

Salii, 50, 84

Sallust, 80

Salus, 78, 153, 190

Salutatio, 36, 198

Saturnalia, 38, 80, 89, 91, 182, 204

Saturnia tellus, 14, 198

Saturnus, 185, 190

Schola Ermetico Pitagorica Italica, 141

Schola Philosofica Hermetica Classica Italica 127, 129

Scylla, 114

Senate, 43, 50, 53, 56, 109, 120

Septemviri epulonum, 50, 198

Septimontium, 9, 17, 198

Serapeum, 130, 198

Serifos, 98

Seven hills of Rome, 3

Sibillini, 50

Sive Supertitio, 198

Socrates, 44, 62, 202

Sodales Augustales, 50

Sodales Titii, 50, 198

Sol, 190

Solar calendar, 55, 166, 169-182

Somnium Scipionis, 43, 80, 198

Soul, 99, 100, 101, 103, 104, 109, 112, 114, 115, 134, 140, 184, 186

Spirit, 74, 76, 89, 101, 103, 104, 112, 114, 116, 186, 197

St. George, 107

Star, 107, 109, 110

Stercutus, 25, 27, 190

Sumerian, 54

Supere, 42, 198

Tarquinius Priscus 28

Tarsus, 98

Temple of Saturn, 14, 21, 190

Temple of Vesta, xi, 5, 13, 31, 32, 57

Templum Apollinis, 141

Templum Iovis, 141

Templum Minervae, 141, 163

The Metamorphosis, 218

The True Word, 62

Thebes, 85

Theodosius, 125, 161

Theogony, 80, 148, 149

Theophilus, 130

Thus, 15, 36, 198

Tiberinus, 10

Troy, 112, 114, 116, 139

University la Sapienza 9, 39

Uranus, 149, 185, 189, 190, 191

Urbe, 5, 13, 39, 152, 185, 198, 201, 202, 203

Vatican, 116

Vaticini, 199

Vediovis, 24, 191

Veio, 14, 152

Velabro, 199

Venus, xiv, 11, 23, 46, 53 , 54, 82, 91, 94, 120, 149, 159, 169, 170, 171, 172, 173, 174, 175, 176, 177, 178, 179, 180, 181, 182, 187, 190, 191, 203, 204

Veritas, 70, 199

Vestal, 9, 20, 31, 32, 54, 56, 57

Via Cutro, 136

Via Romana, 136

Via Sacra, 21, 23, 31, 199, 201

Vigilantes, 56, 199

Vir, 199

Virgo, 65, 76, 170, 199, 203

Viri clarissimi, 50, 199

Virtue, 31, 62, 67, 74, 76, 80, 83, 91, 162, 199

Vis, 199

Visigoths, 15

Vitruvius, 42, 148, 203

Volcanalis, 57

Volturnalis, 57

Vulcanus, 187, 191

WCER, 163

Wisdom, 80

About Author

Giuseppe Barbera is the President of Associazione Tradizionale Pietas and the Pontifex Maximus of the Pietas, the Gentile Community of Roman Religion in Italy. He is the son of Gianfranco Barbera whose students together with Giuseppe founded the organization in 2005. Giuseppe is an archeologist, public speaker and writer focused on the revival and growth of the classical religion of his ancestors in this beautiful country.

Mythology Corner
www.mythologycorner.com

www.ingramcontent.com/pod-product-compliance
Lightning Source LLC
Chambersburg PA
CBHW022057160426
43198CB00008B/262